CHURCHILL

CHURCHILL

Paul Johnson

VIKING

VIKING
Published by the Penguin Group
Penguin Group (USA) Inc., 375 Hudson Street,
New York, New York 10014, U.S.A.
Penguin Group (Canada), 90 Eglinton Avenue East, Suite 700, Toronto,
Ontario, Canada M4P 2Y3 (a division of Pearson Penguin Canada Inc.)
Penguin Books Ltd, 80 Strand, London WC2R 0RL, England
Penguin Ireland, 25 St. Stephen's Green, Dublin 2, Ireland
(a division of Penguin Books Ltd)
Penguin Books Australia Ltd, 250 Camberwell Road, Camberwell,
Victoria 3124, Australia (a division of Pearson Australia Group Pty Ltd)
Penguin Books India Pvt Ltd, 11 Community Centre,
Panchsheel Park, New Delhi–110 017, India
Penguin Group (NZ), 67 Apollo Drive, Rosedale, North Shore 0632,
New Zealand (a division of Pearson New Zealand Ltd)
Penguin Books (South Africa) (Pty) Ltd, 24 Sturdee Avenue,
Rosebank, Johannesburg 2196, South Africa

Penguin Books Ltd, Registered Offices: 80 Strand, London WC2R 0RL, England

First published in 2009 by Viking Penguin, a member of Penguin Group (USA) Inc.

1 3 5 7 9 10 8 6 4 2

Copyright © Paul Johnson, 2009
All rights reserved

Photograph credits appear on pages 169–70.

LIBRARY OF CONGRESS CATALOGING-IN-PUBLICATION DATA
Johnson, Paul, 1928–
Churchill / by Paul Johnson.
p. cm.
Includes bibliographical references and index.
ISBN 978-0-670-02105-5
1. Churchill, Winston, 1874–1965. 2. Prime ministers—Great Britain—Biography.
3. Great Britain—Politics and government—20th century. I. Title.
DA566.9.C5J64 2009
941.084092—dc22
[B]   2009008326

Printed in the United States of America
Set in Bulmer
Designed by Francesca Belanger

This book is dedicated
to my eldest son, Daniel

Contents

Chapter One

Young Thruster

O f all the towering figures of the twentieth century, both good and evil, Winston Churchill was the most valuable to humanity, and also the most likable. It is a joy to write his life, and to read about it. None holds more lessons, especially for youth: How to use a difficult childhood. How to seize eagerly on all opportunities, physical, moral, and intellectual. How to dare greatly, to reinforce success, and to put the inevitable failures behind you. And how, while pursuing vaulting ambition with energy and relish, to cultivate also friendship, generosity, compassion, and decency.

No man did more to preserve freedom and democracy and the values we hold dear in the West. None provided more public entertainment with his dramatic ups and downs, his noble oratory, his powerful writings and sayings, his flashes of rage, and his sunbeams of wit. He took a prominent place on the public stage of his country and the world for over sixty years, and it seemed empty with his departure. Nor has anyone since combined so felicitously such a powerful variety of roles. How did one man do so much, for so long, and so effectively? As a young politician, he found himself sitting at dinner next to Violet Asquith, daughter of the then chancellor of the exchequer. Responding to her question, he announced: "We are all worms. But I really think I am a glow worm." Why did he glow so ardently? Let us inquire.

. . .

Winston Leonard Spencer Churchill was born on November 30, 1874. His parents were Lord Randolph Churchill, younger son of the 7th Duke of Marlborough, and Jennie, second of the four daughters of Leonard Jerome, financier, of Chicago and New York. The birth was due to take place in London, in a Mayfair mansion the young couple had taken, where all was prepared. But during a visit to Blenheim Palace, Lord Randolph's home, Jennie had a fall, and her child was born two months prematurely in a ground-floor bedroom at the palace, hastily got ready. Thus the characteristic note was struck: the unexpected, haste, risk, danger, and drama. The birth pangs were eight hours long and exhausting, but the child was "very healthy," also "wonderfully pretty." He had red hair, described as "the colour of a bronze putter," fair, pink skin, and strong lungs. He later boasted that his skin was exceptionally delicate and forced him always to wear silk next to it. He claimed he had never owned or worn a pair of pajamas in his life. Like his mother, he was active and impulsive and so accident prone, but of organic disease he was little troubled for most of a long life. Though he suffered from deafness in old age, he had no disabilities other than a slight lisp (almost undetectable on recordings). For this reason he took great care of his teeth. He went to the best dentist of his time, Sir Wilfred Fish, who designed his dentures, which were made by the outstanding technician Derek Cudlipp. (They are preserved in London's Royal College of Surgeons Museum.) He also took care of his health, appointing, as soon as he was able, a personal physician, Charles McMoran Wilson, whom he made Lord Moran (Fish was rewarded with a knighthood). Churchill also ate heartily, especially steak, sole, and oysters. He daily sipped large quantities of whiskey or brandy, heavily diluted with water or soda. Despite this, his liver, inspected after his death, was found to be as perfect as a young child's. Churchill was capable of tremendous physical and intellectual efforts, of high intensity over long periods, often with little sleep. But he had corresponding powers of relaxation, filled with a variety of pleasurable occupations, and he also had the gift of taking short naps when time permitted. Again, when possible, he spent his mornings in bed, telephoning, dictating, and receiving visitors. In 1946, when I was seventeen, I had the good fortune to ask him a question: "Mr. Churchill, sir, to what do you attribute your success in life?" Without pause or hesitation, he replied: "Conservation of energy. Never stand up when you can sit down, and never sit down when you can lie down." He then got into his limo.

This vivacious and healthy child was the elder of two sons born to remarkable parents. The father, Lord Randolph Churchill (1849–95), was educated at Eton and Merton College, Oxford. He was MP for the family borough of Woodstock, just outside Blenheim Palace, for the decade 1874–85, and then for South Paddington in London until his death. His political life was meteoric, turbulent, and punctuated by spectacular rows. With a few discontented colleagues, he founded a pressure group advocating more vigorous opposition to the Liberal majority (1880–84) and espousing what he called "Tory Democracy." But, asked what it stood for, he privately replied: "Oh, opportunism, mostly." He also opposed Gladstone's Irish Home Rule policy, which would have made Protestant Ulster submit to an all-Ireland Catholic majority, with the inflammatory slogan "Ulster will fight—and Ulster will be right."

He was an impressive speaker, and by the mid-1880s he was one of only four politicians whose speeches the Central News Agency correspondents had orders to repeat in full, the other three being Gladstone himself, Lord Salisbury, the Tory leader, and the dynamic radical-imperialist Joseph Chamberlain. The years 1885–86 marked the apex of Lord Randolph's career. He was first secretary of state for India, and then for six months chancellor of the exchequer. But while preparing his first budget he had a deadly row over spending with the prime minister. Salisbury was supported by the rest of the cabinet, and Lord Randolph resigned, discovering in the process that he had grotesquely overplayed his hand. It was a case of the dog barking but the caravan moving on. He never recovered from this mistake. At the same time, a mysterious and progressive illness began to affect him. Some believed it was syphilis, others a form of mental corrosion inherited from his mother's branch of the family, the Londonderrys. Gradually his speeches became confused and halting and painful to listen to, until death in 1895 drew a merciful curtain over his shattered career. Winston was only twenty when his father died, and was haunted by this tragic final phase until he exorcised the ghost by writing a magnificent two-volume biography, transforming his father into one of the great tragic figures of English political history. It was a further source of unhappiness for Winston that he had seen so little of his father, first so busy, then so stricken. He remembered every word of the few personal conversations he had had with him.

How much Winston inherited from his father, good or bad, is a matter of opinion. Mine is: not much. Indeed there was little of the Churchills in him. They were, on the whole, an unremarkable lot. Even the founder, John, 1st Duke of Marlborough, might, in the view of King Charles II, a shrewd judge of men, have remained a quiet country gentleman had he not been stirred into activity by his astounding and ambitious wife, Sarah Jennings. Of his successors, none achieved distinction. Five of the first seven dukes were victims of pathological depression. Winston, it is true, complained of periodic dark moods, which he called "the Black Dog." But these were occasioned by actual reverses, and were soon dispersed by vigorous activity. His father's extremism and his judgments were often quoted against him during his own career, and there were a few occasions when he went too far and was severely punished for it. But in general, he learned from Lord Randolph's mistakes and pulled back from the brink. Nor was there ever any sign of the mental breakdown which slowly took possession of his father. Until his late eighties, Winston remained in full possession of his faculties despite a general physical decline.

It was, rather, from his mother that Winston derived his salient characteristics: energy, a love of adventure, ambition, a sinuous intellect, warm feelings, courage and resilience, and a huge passion for life in all its aspects. His aim to be the most important politician in Westminster was a male projection of her intense desire to be the desirable lady in Mayfair. She kept and held this title for a decade or more, not just because of the sheer physical allure of face and figure but because she looked, moved, talked, laughed, and danced with almost diabolical magic. She said later: "I shall never get used to not being the most beautiful woman in the room." It was an intoxication to sweep in and know every man had turned his head. She was also very much an American. She believed the sky was the limit, that everything was possible, that tradition, precedents, the "right" way of doing things could always be ignored when ambition demanded. She loved high risks and did not weep—for long, anyway—if they did not come off. All this she transmitted to her firstborn son (Winston's younger brother, Jack, brought up from infancy playing second fiddle, was much more of a routine Churchill). She also accustomed him to be the center of conversation. In the mid-1870s the Churchills went into exile in Dublin after Lord Randolph, characteristically, took violent sides with his elder brother over a woman and antagonized the Prince of Wales. The Duke of Marlborough had hastily to be appointed viceroy of Ireland, and thither the Churchills went, to electrify Dublin Castle, until the storm blew over. Winston's earliest memory was of his grandfather, then viceroy, haranguing the elite in the courtyard of their castle. The subject: war. Winston saw little of his parents, then and later. The principal figure of his childhood was Mrs. Elizabeth Anne Everest (1833–95), his nurse, a Kentish woman of humble background who loved him passionately and whom he knew as "Woomany" or "Woom." Her letters to him are touching period pieces. He returned her affection and memorialized her in his novel, *Savrola,* which contains a powerful passage praising the virtues and loyalty of family servants. Her existence and love ensured that Winston's childhood, which might have been disastrous and destructive of him, was reasonably happy.

The Everest-Winston relationship was one of the best episodes in Churchill's entire life. She encouraged and comforted him throughout his school days in ways his mother could not or would not, detecting in him both his genius and his loving nature. He responded by cherishing her as his closest confidante in all his anxieties. He believed his parents treated her meanly, dismissing her after her services were no longer needed and leaving her to a life of poverty. Though still a schoolboy, he did his best to alleviate her privations, and later he sent her money when he could afford it. He attended her deathbed, and took Jack with him to the funeral. He had inscribed and set up her headstone and paid a local florist annually to ensure that her grave was kept up.

Winston loved both his parents with the limitless, irrational love of a passionate child and adolescent. But they continually disappointed him, by absence, indifference, and reproaches. He was not a boy who did naturally well at school and his reports were mediocre. His father soon wrote him off as an academic failure. After his poor performance at private school Lord Randolph decided not to send him to Eton: not clever enough. Instead he was put down for Harrow. One day he visited Winston's playroom, where the boy's collection of lead soldiers was set out. There were over a thousand of them, organized as an infantry division with a cavalry brigade. (Jack had an "enemy" army, but its soldiers were all black men, and it was not permitted to possess artillery.) Lord Randolph inspected Winston's troops and asked if he would like an army career, thinking "that is all he is fit for." Winston, believing his father's question meant he foresaw for his son a life of glory and victory in the Marlborough tradition, answered enthusiastically, "Yes." So it was settled.

Winston's performance at Harrow confirmed his father's belief he would come to no good. He never got out of the bottom form, spending three years there, until he was transferred to the Army Class, to prepare him for the Cadet School at Sandhurst. Some of Lord Randolph's letters to him are crushing, indeed brutal. His mother's are more loving but they too often reflect his father's discontent. Few schoolboys can ever have received such discouraging letters from their parents. His father, too, was determined Winston should go into the infantry, while Winston preferred the cavalry. The infantry required higher marks but it was cheaper. His parents, especially Lord Randolph, were worried about money. He had an income from the Blenheim estates, and his wife brought with her another from her father. But together they scarcely covered the expenses of a fashionable couple in high society; they had no savings and debts accumulated. Winston contrived, just, to get into Sandhurst on his third attempt, and he did reasonably well, true. But he went into the cavalry—the Fourth Hussars—to his father's fury. But by this time Lord Randolph was nearing the end. He went to South Africa in an attempt to make a fortune for his family in the gold and diamond fields. In fact he was guided into shrewd investments, which would eventually have proved very valuable. But when he died in 1895, all had to be sold to pay his debts. It was clear by then that Winston would have to earn his own living.

As it happened, Harrow proved invaluable in enabling him to do so. He did not acquire fluency in the Latin and Greek it provided so plentifully. He learned a few trusty Latin quotations and skill at putting them to use. But he noticed that his headmaster, the Reverend J. E. C. Welldon (later his friend as bishop of Calcutta), winced as he pronounced them, and he perceived, later, the same expression cross the face of Prime Minister Asquith, a noted classical scholar, when he pronounced a Latin quote in cabinet. But if he never became a classicist, he achieved something much more worthwhile and valuable: fluency in the English language, written and spoken. Three years in the bottom form, under the eager tuition of the English master, Robert Somervell, made this possible. Winston became not merely adept but masterly in his use of words. And he loved them. They became the verbal current coursing through his veins as he shaped his political manhood. No English statesman has ever loved them more or made more persistent use of them to forward his career and redeem it in time of trouble. Words were also his main source of income throughout his life, from the age of twenty-one. Almost from the start he was unusually well paid, and his books eventually made prodigious sums for himself and his descendants. He wrote thousands of articles for newspapers and magazines and over forty books. Some were very long. His account of the Second World War is over 2,050,000 words. Gibbon's *Decline and Fall of the Roman Empire* by comparison is 1,100,000 words. I calculate his total of words in print, including published speeches, to be between 8 and 10 million. There can have been few boys who made such profitable use of something learned at school. In that sense, Winston's education, contrary to the traditional view, was a notable success.

In the process of turning words into cash, Lady Randolph played a key part, particularly in getting her son commissions. She had done all she could to alleviate Lord Randolph's suffering in his slow and dreadful decline. But after his death in 1895, she was free to devote herself to furthering her elder son's career, and this became the object of all her exertions. In begging for help for Winston she was fearless, shameless, persistent, and almost always successful. Her position in London society, her beauty and charm, and her cunning enabled her to worm her way into the good books of newspaper proprietors and editors, publishers and politicians—anyone in a position to help. "This is a pushing age," Winston wrote to her, "and we must push with the best." They became the pushiest couple in London, indeed in the empire, which then spread over nearly a quarter of the earth's surface.

No sooner commissioned into the army, Churchill (as we may now call him) began his plan of campaign to make himself famous, or at least conspicuous. A soldier needs war, and Churchill needed it more than most, for he could turn war into words, and so into cash. But if you sat still, expecting wars to come to you, you might be starved of action. You had to go to the wars. That became Churchill's policy. The Fourth Hussars, under Colonel Brabazon, a family friend, was ordered to India. But there was a handsome war going on in Cuba, where America had sympathy for the insurgents. Brabazon's agreement was reluctantly secured, and Churchill and his mother pulled strings to get him to the front and arranged a contract with the *Daily Graphic* to publish his dispatches. By November 1895 he was already under fire as well as braving outbreaks of yellow fever and smallpox. "For the first time," he wrote, "I heard shots fired in anger and heard bullets strike flesh or whistle through the air." This recalls the famous description by George Washington of first hearing bullets whistle in 1757. But unlike Washington, Churchill did not find "something pleasant in the sound." On the contrary, he learned to take cover. He was under fire, I calculate, about fifty times in the course of his life, and never once hit by a bullet. He was not the only outsider who came to Cuba for experience. Theodore Roosevelt, his older contemporary, led a force of freebooters there. The two men had a great deal in common but did not get on. Roosevelt said: "That young man Churchill is not a gentleman. He does not rise to his feet when a lady enters the room." That may be true. Once Churchill was comfortably ensconced in a chair, he was reluctant to rise, part of his conservation-of-energy principle.

The Spaniards awarded Churchill their standard medal for officers, the Red Cross, which he gratefully received—his first medal—along with twenty-five guineas paid by the *Graphic* for five articles. Thus the pattern of his life for the next five years was set. Finding wars. Getting special permission to visit or participate in them. Reporting them for newspapers and in book form. And collecting medals. Once in India, he looked about him for action. But he was not idle while waiting for opportunities. He was conscious of his ignorance and begged his mother to send him big, important books. She did. The Indian army day began early but there was a big gap in the middle when the sun was hottest. Most spent it in siesta. Churchill read. He thus devoured Macaulay's *History of England* and Gibbon. He also read Winwood Reade's atheistic tract, *The Martyrdom of Man,* which turned him into a lifelong freethinker and a critic of organized religion (though he always conformed outwardly enough to avoid the label "atheist," which might have been politically damaging). He read everything of value he could get his hands on, and forgot nothing he read. But there were always gaps, he felt, in his knowledge, which he eagerly filled when vital books were recommended to him.

In August 1897 he took part in his first British campaign, as a member of the Malakand Field Force raised by Sir Bindon Blood to punish the Pathans for incursion. Blood was a glamorous figure, a descendant of the Colonel Blood who tried to steal the Crown Jewels under Charles II. The expedition was a notable success, and Churchill saw action, was under fire, and learned a good deal about punitive expeditions and guerrilla warfare. His mother arranged for him to write for the *Daily Telegraph* a series of "letters." He was annoyed with her for not first stipulating they be signed—for he was hot on the scent of fame—and he demanded £100 for the series. He also wrote for the Indian paper *The Allahabad Pioneer* and eventually a book, *The Story of the Malakand Field Force*. This was his first book, and he sent a copy to the Prince of Wales, who wrote him a delightful letter of thanks, praised it to the skies, and recommended it to all his friends. Blood was also pleased with him and reported favorably to his superiors. He lived to a great age, dying in 1940, two days after he received the glorious news that his former subaltern had become prime minister. Churchill followed up this success with attachment to the Tirah Expeditionary Force: more experience, another medal.

Churchill was already looking to Africa, which in 1897 was alive with wars, actual and threatened. He wrote to his mother, which tersely and crudely exposed his aim to use fame in war to get himself into Parliament: "A few months in South Africa would earn me the SA medal and in all probability the Company's Star. Thence hot-foot to Egypt—to return with two more decorations in a year or two—and beat my sword into an iron dispatch box." Actually, it was Egypt which came first. With tremendous efforts, Lady Randolph got him attached to a cavalry regiment taking part in the expedition to avenge Gordon's murder at Khartoum. This involved an appeal to the prime minister, over the head of the local commander in chief, Lord Kitchener, who had already heard of Churchill's growing reputation as a pushy medal chaser and did not want him. Nevertheless the young man arrived in time to take part in one of the last cavalry charges in the history of the British army, during the famous battle of Omdurman (1899), which destroyed the Dervish army. Churchill reported this campaign, too, for the London press, for handsome payment, and also produced one of his best books, *The River War,* in two volumes, a magnificent account of the splendors and horrors of imperialism at its zenith.

Next came South Africa, where he reported the Boer War for the *Morning Post.* Strictly speaking he was a noncombatant, but during a Boer ambush of an armored train, he took an active part, characteristically directing operations to free the engine. He was captured, made a prisoner of war, escaped, had a hazardous journey through the Boer lines, with posters advertising a large reward for his recapture, and had a rapturous welcome in Durban, where he found himself a hero. He then went back to the war in earnest, showing an extraordinary amount of physical energy. Before the Boers surrendered Johannesburg, Churchill contrived to tour the city on bicycle, speeding up when he saw armed parties of the enemy. We tend to epitomize Churchill by his later sedentary existence. In youth he was hyperactive. He was the Harrow and Public Schools Fencing Champion—and fencing is one of the most energetic of sports. In India he played polo enthusiastically, being part of his regimental team, which won the All-India Calcutta Cup, the supreme prize in those days. Much of his time in South Africa was spent on his tramping feet, wearing out a pair of boots in the process. He was among thirty thousand men who marched in triumph to Pretoria, the Boer capital, led by a war balloon which he compared in his *Morning Post* report to "the pillar of cloud which led the hosts of Israel."

All his exploits figured largely in his newspaper articles. But by

1900 he felt he had exhausted the opportunities of South Africa, where the war had settled into an exacting but dull guerrilla campaign. He hurried home. He had achieved the fame he sought, made himself conspicuous (his photograph appeared over a hundred times in newspapers in the year 1900), and returned to London a hero. He quickly published two books, *London to Ladysmith via Pretoria* and *Ian Hamilton's March*. Cashing in further on his fame, he gave a series of public lectures in Britain, Canada, and the United States. These efforts left him with a capital of £10,000, which was invested for him by his father's financial adviser, Sir Ernest Cassel. In addition, he had a row of medals: the Spanish Cross of the Order of Military Merit, First Class; the India Medal 1895, with clasp; the Queen's Sudan Medal 1896–98, no clasp; the Khedive's Sudan Medal, with clasp; and the Queen's South Africa Medal, with six clasps. He also earned the Cuban Campaign Medal 1895–98 from Spain. He had meanwhile taken his first steps in politics. He contested Oldham for the Tories in 1899, and won it in the "khaki election" the following year. In all these rapid developments, he had accumulated a number of critics and even enemies, and a reputation for being brash, arrogant, presumptuous, disobedient, boastful, and a bounder. He was accused of abusing his position as a British officer and his civilian status as a journalist, and of breaking his word of honor as a war prisoner. Among the orthodox and "right thinking," the mention of his name raised hackles. On the other hand he was the best-known young man of his generation. When he took the corner seat above the gangway in the House of Commons to make his maiden speech in February 1901—it was the seat occupied by his father for his resignation speech in 1886—he was barely twenty-six. It was not bad going.

Chapter Two

Liberal Statesman

Churchill was now in the House of Commons. But what for? Personal advancement, certainly. He thirsted for office, power, and the chance to make history. Personal vindication, too: to avenge his father's failure by becoming prime minister himself. But were there not higher motives? Did not altruistic elements co-exist with his ambition, vanity, and lust for success? Did he have a political philosophy? A book has been written on the subject but leaves one little wiser. Churchill, then and always, was a mass of contradictions.

Churchill's experiences as a young warrior confirmed and intensified his imperialism. The empire was a splendid thing: enormous, world-embracing, seemingly all-powerful, certainly gorgeously colorful, exciting, offering dazzling opportunities for the progress and fulfillment of all races, provided the white elite who ran it kept their nerve and self-confidence. Churchill never lacked either and was anxious to display them in ruling an empire whose outward show stood for everything he loved and enjoyed. He also had certain gut instincts which fitted in well at a time when the great-power "scramble for Africa" was at its height. From the Sudan in 1899 he wrote to his mother: "I have a keen aboriginal desire to kill some of these odious dervishes . . . I anticipate enjoying the exercise very much."

At the same time Churchill had a warm and tender heart and a perceptive insight into the darker side of power. He saw the horror of empire as well as its splendor. He loved to be top dog. But he felt for the underdog. *The River War,* for instance, was an accurate and unflinching account of what he saw. He told his cousin Ivor Guest: "I do not think the book will bring me many friends, [but] in writing the great thing is to be honest." It angered Kitchener and many others, another item in the growing dossier of "Churchill's unreliability." The official reports after Omdurman said the wounded Dervishes "received every attention." In fact, he told his mother, their treatment was disgraceful and most were just slaughtered. Kitchener, he told her, was "a vulgar, common man—without much of the non-brutal elements in his composition." This was toned down in the book. Even so, he dealt with the question of the wounded Dervishes honestly, and he added: "The stern and unpitying spirit of the commander was communicated to his troops." In a sense, he disapproved of the whole expedition insofar as it was a gigantic reprisal for the murder of Gordon. He wrote: "It may be that the gods forbad vengeance to man because they reserved for themselves so intoxicating a drink. But the cup should not be drained to the bottom. The dregs are often filthy tasting."

It would be untrue to say that Churchill, as a young politician and junior minister at the Colonial Office, kept an eagle eye open for the blemishes of empire. But when they attracted his attention he spoke out. He expressed his concern for the six hundred Tibetans killed by the machine guns of the Younghusband expedition to Lhasa, and for the twenty-five Zulu rebels deported to Saint Helena and who, he said, were starving there. He was quick to speak out for the Boers in giving a generous peace and reconciliation. In his maiden speech in the Commons, made immediately after taking the oath, his opening words were: "If I were a Boer, I hope I should be fighting in the field." This was not the least courageous of the five hundred major speeches he was to make in the Commons over the next sixty years. Nor did his eagerness to see war, and the relish he took in it and in medal collecting, blind him to its inescapable horrors, or prevent him from taking every opportunity to warn fellow MPs about its nature. In another speech in his first year in Parliament, he said that colonial wars were beastly, marked by atrocities and senseless slaughters. But a European war would be infinitely worse. He was "alarmed," he said, by the "composure," even "glibness," with which MPs and, worse, ministers talked of a possible European war: "A European war cannot be anything but a cruel, heart-rending struggle, which, if we are ever to enjoy the bitter fruits of victory, must demand, perhaps for several years, the whole manhood of the nation, the entire suspension of peaceful industries, and the concentration, to one end, of every vital energy in the community." He added: "Democracy is more vindictive than Cabinets. The wars of peoples will be more terrible than the wars of kings." These prophetic words were spoken more than a dozen years before the catastrophe occurred in 1914. Churchill was never a warmonger as his enemies claimed. On the contrary: he warned against it just as urgently as he warned against unpreparedness for it—the two were indivisible. But Churchill was sufficient of a realist to grasp that wars will come, and that a victorious one, however dreadful, is preferable to a lost one.

In a broader sense, it is not easy to classify Churchill. He had a historian's mind, eager to grapple with facts, actualities, to answer the who, how, where, when questions, rather than a philosopher's, mesmerized by abstractions with their whys and wherefores. He was born a Tory and entered Parliament as one. But he was unhappy on the Tories' benches. Salisbury, the man who had destroyed his father, ceased to be leader in 1902 but, on retiring, handed over to his nephew, A. J. Balfour, cool, aloof, calculating rather than impulsive. Now, *he* had a philosopher's mind, and Churchill found it uncongenial, although they moved in similar circles and remained nominally friends until Balfour's death in 1930. Churchill had no desire to serve under him. Moreover, Balfour had got himself and his party into a muddle over free trade; Joe Chamberlain, having split the old Liberal Party over Ireland in 1886, now split the Tories over his plan to reimpose protective tariffs. Churchill's constituency, Oldham, was a free trade town and he was, too, both by interest and by choice. Moreover, it was really a Liberal seat which he had won by a fluke in the "khaki" landslide of 1900, and he was more likely to hold it as a Liberal. The Tories had been predominant for twenty years but the wind of change was now blowing and the young man, sniffing it, wanted it to fill his sails. So he "crossed over" in 1904 and fought and won Oldham as a Liberal in the 1906 election, which returned a huge Liberal majority. This caused fury among the right-thinking, and they added a hefty item to Churchill's dossier of unreliability.

He was not a party man. That was the truth. His loyalty belonged to the national interest, and his own. At one time or another he stood for Parliament under six labels: Conservative, Liberal, Coalition, Constitutionalist, Unionist, and National Conservative. This was partly due to his failure to find a safe seat, or one he could hold. For his first quarter century in the Commons he moved between Oldham (1900–1906), North-West Manchester (1906–8), and Dundee, which he scrambled into in 1908 and finally lost in 1922, being then outside the Commons for over a year. This dictated his return to the Conservatives. He said: "Anyone can rat. It takes real skill to re-rat." His reward was that he at last got a safe seat he could hold in all seasons, Epping in Essex (later called Woodford), which he retained for thirty-five years, once as a Constitutionalist, twice as a Unionist, once as a National Conservative, and five times as a simple Conservative, usually with enormous majorities. This safe seat, near London, was of enormous benefit to his career. He never had to worry about it.

All the same, if Churchill was ever anything, he was a Liberal (as well as a traditionalist and a small-c conservative). There is a curious story about this, told to me by the Labour MP "Curly" Mallalieu in 1962, when Churchill was in his eighties, though still an MP. There is, or was, a curious contraption called the "House of Lords Lift" in which peers were elevated to the upper floor of Parliament, mere MPs being allowed to use it only if injured or decrepit. Churchill had permanent permission, and Curly had hurt himself playing football. One day when he got in he found Churchill there. The old man glared and said: "Who are you?" "I'm Bill Mallalieu, sir, MP for Huddersfield." "What party?" "Labour, sir." "Ah. I'm a Liberal. *Always have been.*" The fiendish glee with which he made this remark was memorable.

Churchill's courage in crossing the floor made him a marked man, and it was no surprise when the prime minister, Sir Henry Campbell-Bannerman, made him undersecretary to the colonies in

1905. He was only thirty-one, and the office was important, for his boss, Lord Elgin, was in the Lords, and Churchill had to do all the Commons business covering the entire world himself, and stand up to the Tory heavyweights, including Joe Chamberlain, the first to make the colonies a fashionable, key job, the road to the top. But standing up to this opposition from the front bench was precisely what Churchill was good at, then and always. He was fluent, resourceful, witty, and always well briefed. He enjoyed himself on his feet and did his best to interest, even enthrall, and always to entertain the House with his sallies and jokes, his moments of indignation, real or simulated, his obvious love of words and the relish with which he brought them out, not least his huge pleasure in the rituals of the Commons and his reverence for its traditions. Members always love those who love the House, and Churchill plainly did.

He also loved his job, with its telegrams, king's messengers in uniform, red leather dispatch boxes, and important visitors, black, yellow, and white, from all over the world. He was certainly conspicuous. His name came up in a conversation between Rudyard Kipling, the Orpheus of the empire, and one of its greatest builders, Cecil Rhodes—how one wishes a transcript had survived. Churchill paid an official visit to the East African colonies in 1907, traveling with his devoted secretary "Eddie" Marsh, a fixture in his official life for the next twenty-five years. Going up from the coast to the Ugandan plateau by the new railway, Churchill described it as "like travelling up the beanstalk into fairyland." He made the most of the trip uphill by standing on the cowcatcher of the engine as it puffed its way through the jungle, a typical Churchill touch of vainglory which duly made its way into the newspapers and caused tut-tutting. In Uganda and Kenya he went on safari with Marsh and 350 porters. In India he had stuck wild pig but could not afford big game. Now he shot rhino, zebra, wildebeest, and gazelle, sending his trophies back to London to be stuffed and mounted by the leading taxidermist, Rowland Ward of Piccadilly. Oddly enough, through a characteristic piece of Churchillian expediency, to avoid criticism of misuse of public funds the trip had been paid for by the *Strand Magazine,* and in return he wrote articles which, extended to book form, became *My African Journey.* Like so many of his activities, this combination of office with journalism would be impossible now. Indeed, it raised eyebrows at the time.

Churchill had become a Privy Counsellor that year; and the next, when H. H. Asquith succeeded "C-B" as prime minister, he was brought into the cabinet. Going to the Colonial Office had been Churchill's idea. He had originally been offered the plum job of financial secretary to the treasury, but he had preferred to work off his global ideas for the colonies (his book is full of schemes for industrializing Africa and harnessing the Nile). Now, however, he wanted to get his teeth into home politics and eagerly accepted Asquith's invitation to succeed Lloyd George, who was promoted to chancellor of the exchequer, as president of the Board of Trade. It was dazzling to reach cabinet rank when only thirty-four, and the post also brought the opportunity to work with LG, with whom he forged a precarious friendship and a more solid policy alliance to bring about an English version of the "welfare state" Bismarck had introduced in Germany.

Churchill realized he was about to embark on his first major adventure in politics, and he wanted to put his private life in order. He had already (January 2, 1906) paid his debt to his family by publishing his magnificent *Lord Randolph Churchill*. As his cousin Ivor Guest put it, "Few fathers had done less for their sons. Few sons have done more for their fathers." Now he wanted a family of his own. An eligible bachelor, he had dutifully fallen in love with various girls, or thought he had, and waltzed around Mayfair ballrooms. But he made little effort to dance in step: not his line. "I trod on the Prince of Wales's toe," he recorded complacently, "and heard him yelp." In August 1908 he proposed to Clementine Hozier, daughter of the late Colonel Sir Henry Hozier, secretary of Lloyd's. Other girls had set their caps at him, including Asquith's daughter Violet, and some of them had substantial *dots*. But Clemmie suited him, and he loved her. He always put happiness before money. Anyway, he never had any doubt he could earn anything required. As he laid down, "Income should be expanded to meet expenditure." They were quickly married, at St. Margaret's, Westminster, Parliament's parish church, in September, and the event was not allowed to crowd out political activities. His best man was the fiercest of England's political tribe, Lord Hugh Cecil, head of the Tory "ultra" pressure group known as the Hughligans, and in the vestry, while the registers were being signed, Churchill had time to have a plotting whisper with LG. He used the honeymoon to complete and dispatch to the printers his African book.

Among all the twentieth-century ruling elites, the Churchills must be judged to have had the most successful marriage. It can be said with reasonable certitude that each was totally faithful to the other. She devoted herself completely to her remarkable husband, gave him much good (usually liberal) advice, which was not always taken, comforted him in his many career mishaps, and calmed him down when he was triumphant. "He always insists I am by him," she said, "and then promptly forgets my existence." True, but he never looked at another woman. They had one son, Randolph, and four daughters, Diana, Sarah, Marigold (who died in infancy), and Mary.

The marital fidelity of the Churchills was a remarkable fact, for the way the Commons works tends to erode vows on both sides. Then, too, both parties had promiscuous mothers. Lady Blanche Hozier, daughter of the Earl of Airlie, had many lovers while her husband was still alive, nine at one time, it was said. Clemmie was not Hozier's daughter but there is no certainty who her father was. The most likely candidate was a flirtatious cavalry officer, "Bay" Middleton, but another possibility was Bertram Mitford, 1st Baron Redesdale, Nancy Mitford's grandfather. If so, it is curious to think that Mrs. Churchill was her aunt. Jennie Churchill also had a number of lovers while Lord Randolph was still alive, and they may even have included Middleton. After Lord Randolph's death she had more, and then made two marriages to younger men, before having one of her falls, through wearing ultrahigh heels, which led to mortification, amputation of her leg, and death (in 1921). There is no doubt Churchill was the son of Lord Randolph. But it is a remarkable fact that the children of such persistent adulteresses should have made such a faithful couple. Given Churchill's adventurous and reckless nature, and his appetite for sensation, his fidelity is notable. It may be that he put all his energy into his political life. Certainly, the marriage was spared many of the irritating rubs of close proximity, for Churchill's hours—up late arguing with colleagues, rising at lunchtime after working in bed—meant that they led separate existences under the same roof: they each had their own bedroom, right from the start. Whatever the reason, fidelity was a godsend and an important contributing factor to Churchill's success, for he was saved all the worry and emotional storm which adultery provokes.

Churchill delighted in his marriage. He was a happy man. Against this background, the years from 1908 proved the most fruitful of his life in terms of the legislation, on the whole highly successful, which he pushed through Parliament. These had the overriding aim of helping the poor, the unemployed, and the lower-paid working class. They included the Trade Boards Act (1909), ending "sweated labour"; the establishment of labor exchanges, to enable employees to fill jobs more quickly; the first National Insurance Act (1911), to provide unemployment pay; allowances for children to set against income tax; the Mines Act (1911), which transformed conditions in the chronically unhappy coal trade; and the Shops Act, which eventually helped shop assistants by requiring a tea break and imposing early closing. For the first time millions of lower-paid workers got a weekly half holiday. Churchill supervised every detail of this extremely complex program, defending it clause by clause in the Commons. He was impelled by a genuine passion for the least fortunate members of society, by a strong belief that society could be made both humane and more efficient, and by his feeling that revolution, of which there were rumblings all over the world at this time, could only be averted by judicious reforms. Other countries were introducing changes, but for a comparable achievement one has to look to the domestic program of Woodrow Wilson in the United States. Churchill's reforms were not his work alone. For the first time he demonstrated his wonderful ability to galvanize civil servants into furious activity and dramatic innovations, and his equal skill in bringing to Whitehall brilliant outsiders, such as William Beveridge, who ran the new labor exchanges and who was later to produce the famous Beveridge Report (1943), the plan on which Britain's welfare state was completed.

Of course, the political giant behind the reforms was the chancellor of the exchequer, Lloyd George, who provided the money. The introduction of old-age pensions in particular—which struck people at the time as the most sensational of the novelties—was his achievement. But Churchill supported him passionately, having the case of Mrs. Everest in his mind: he was always most strongly motivated by personal experience and individual cases. The two worked together to bring the great fleet of measures into harbor, wafted by the winds of their oratory. As speakers they were very different. Churchill had always prepared his set speeches carefully but not word for word. In 1904, however, he had the horrible experience of "drying up" in the Commons, when apparently in full flow. Thereafter he learned everything by heart, rehearsed and timed himself, and left nothing to chance. The Commons was, as a rule, a rapt audience. Lloyd George was an inspirational leader on the Welsh preacher model. He thought and spoke on his feet, and expected the House to interrupt, to participate, and so to inspire sallies, jokes, splashes of venom, and apothegms. He created dramatic pauses and raised hubbubs. So his speaking rate was slower measured in words delivered per minute—85 to Churchill's 111, with Gladstone's 100 as the standard. But the excitement of a Lloyd George speech was intense: you did not know what he would say, and often it came as a surprise, even to the speaker. Later in his life Churchill had to compete for the title of best Commons orator with another Welshman, Aneurin Bevan, who like LG often thought on his feet and was capable of devastating impromptus, especially to interrupters. When I heard both men in the 1950s, I rated Bevan more highly; and Sir Robert Boothby, who was Churchill's parliamentary private secretary in the twenties, close to Lloyd George, and a friend and drinking companion of Bevan's, told me that LG was the best of the three at actually moving the House and changing opinions. However, Churchill's method was right for him and proved invaluable when, in due course, he addressed vast audiences, worldwide, in solemn settings. Moreover, while LG's speeches do not read particularly well (nor do Bevan's), Churchill's orations, in print, usually carry all the resonance of his voice with them: they are magnificent prose, too.

If Churchill and LG carried through a peaceful revolution together, they were not equals. To LG, the radical by birth, upbringing, race, emotional instinct, and voracious appetite for change, to thrust down the mighty from their seats and exalt the poor was his religion and his delight. Both he and Churchill opposed the overambitious race with Germany to build the most battleships. But only LG could, and did, say, "Dukes are more expensive than Dreadnoughts, and often more dangerous!"

Churchill was carried forward by intellectual conviction, but his reverence for tradition acted as a brake, and LG delighted in taunting him about his burden of "strawberry leaves and Blenheim." Inverting the usual hierarchy, he had a superior social position to Churchill, which reinforced his seniority in years, parliamentary experience, and honed political skills. So he was by far the senior partner. Churchill saw it in even more ignominious terms, especially in retrospect. In the mid-1920s, when Churchill was riding high as chancellor of the exchequer, and LG was out of office, for good as it turned out, Boothby sought to heal the breach between the two men—they had scarcely spoken since LG's government broke up in 1922—by bringing the Welshman to Churchill's private room at the Commons for a private chat. After LG slipped away, Boothby went in and found Churchill slumped in somber thought. "Well, how did it go?" "Oh, very well. Within five minutes we were right back in our old relationship." "What was that?" *"Master and servant."*

At the time Churchill was too busy and excited to worry about his subservience, for his horizons continued to expand. In 1910 he was promoted to home secretary. This gave added weight to his role in the reform program but also allowed him to take direct action. All his life he refused to be bound to a desk. He insisted on seeing for himself. His imprisonment by the Boers had given him a horror of confinement, so he visited prisons, conferred with wardens, talked to prisoners alone—probably the first home secretary to do so—and introduced administrative changes, such as regular supplies of books and entertainment. He began the process whereby the incarceration of children was ended. His approach aroused irritation among the possessing classes. Among his duties as home secretary was to send a daily written report to the king when Parliament was sitting. Edward VII had always enjoyed Churchill's jokes and often irreverent approach to politics. George V, who succeeded him in 1910, was less sure of himself, had a much cruder sense of humor, and never could quite see the point of Churchill. His racy letters often appeared improper to the new king. In November 1911 the home secretary wrote that his office was considering labor colonies to deal with "tramps and wastrels." He added: "It must not, however, be forgotten that there are idlers and wastrels at both ends of the social scale." This produced an explosion of anger in the king, who accused the author of "very socialistic views." But Churchill, who was never content to be silent or inactive when the opportunity to say or do something interesting presented itself, got into trouble with the Socialists and their trade union allies, too. A miners' strike at Tonypandy in the Rhondda Valley of South Wales threatened to be beyond the powers of the local police to control. Churchill ordered troops to the area as a deterrent. This was a bold thing to do, bound to arouse resentment among both militant trade unionists and Tory armchair critics who disliked Churchillian "theatricals" as they called them—two excellent reasons, in his view, why he should do it. In fact it succeeded. The police were able to disperse the miners by using their rolled-up mackintoshes—they did not even need to draw their truncheons. The general on the spot, Neville Macready, testified: "It was entirely due to Mr. Churchill's forethought that bloodshed was avoided." But the accusation was made and persisted—it still does among trade unionists—that Churchill ordered the army to fire on the miners. "Remember Tonypandy" was a bitter hustings cry used against Churchill at every election thereafter.

A more sensational episode followed. The British were used to Irish "outrages" but in the years before the wars they had to put up with a new menace, international terrorists termed anarchists. The phenomenon is well treated in Conrad's novel *Under Western Eyes*.

Among those ranked as anarchists were a gang of Latvian immigrants under a man called Peter the Painter. They had already killed three policemen while tunneling into a jeweler's shop, and in January 1911 they were holed up in a house in Sidney Street in London's East End. Churchill was advised to send a party of Scots Guards from the Tower of London to help the police. He was delighted to agree, and went also in person to see the "siege," dragging with him Eddie Marsh, the poetry lover and art collector out of office hours, who was terrified. Photographers were present and the newspapers showed the home secretary, apparently directing police and soldiers, wearing a top hat and a beautiful coat with fur lining and astrakhan collar. When a fire broke out in the besieged house he certainly gave orders to the fire brigade: "Let it burn." Two charred bodies were later found in the ruins. Balfour, who never did anything active if he could help it (except to play golf), asked maliciously in the Commons, "I understand what the photographer was doing. But what was the Right Honourable Gentleman doing?" This episode became another weighty item in the anti-Churchill dossier, and the photo of Churchill at the siege was reproduced thousands of times, and still is. Hard to see, today, what he did wrong. A minister with direct experience of how violent crime is handled is of more use than one who merely reads reports. Besides, Churchill enjoyed it: he assured his colleague Charles Masterman, "It was such fun." When a fuss was made about corporal punishment of criminals, and various specially designed rods and birches were produced, Churchill and Eddie Marsh flogged themselves with them in the home secretary's office. That was fun, too. As such it was in contrast to his general experience as home secretary, which he found grim: "Of all the offices I have held," he told a newspaper in the midthirties, "this was the one I liked least." He particularly disliked exercising the power of the home secretary to confirm death sentences or commute them to life imprisonment. Of the forty-three cases that came before him, he commuted twenty-one. Churchill was never a supporter of abolition of capital punishment. He thought long incarceration much more horrible. But the night before a hanging he brooded on the condemned man's fate: it was one of the very few worries which ever robbed him of his sleep.

All the same, Churchill later admitted that he relished the years before the First World War more than any other period of his career. We tend to think of them as a halcyon age of peace, prosperity, and pleasure, the last in English history. In fact it was an age of turbulence, and that is one reason Churchill enjoyed it so much. It was not the world war which ended the ancien régime but the years before it: the war was merely one of the symptoms of the change. There is a remarkable book, *The Strange Death of Liberal England,* in which George Dangerfield presents the epoch in this light, a time of frenzy, extremism, and incipient violence, banishing the old Liberal slogan of "Peace, Prosperity and Reform," and with it all tranquillity in public life. The unions were active as never before, taking full advantage of their virtual immunity to actions for damages caused by strikes, which the Liberals had unwisely conferred on them in 1906. The suffragettes were turning from protest to direct action, were being brutally arrested, sent to prison, and forcibly fed when they resorted to hunger strikes. In 1909, to pay for the welfare state, Lloyd George introduced a budget which taxed land values, so hitting hard the aristocracy, and increased taxation generally.

Breaking a long tradition under which the House of Lords automatically passed finance bills agreed by the Commons, the Lords rejected it, the Tories using their overwhelming built-in majority there. Asquith had either to withdraw or tone down the budget, to create peers to enable it to be passed—which King George initially declined to do—or to go to the country. But two elections in 1910 failed to decide the matter, though they robbed the Liberals of their huge majority over all parties, forcing Asquith to rely on Irish support in order to go on governing. That in turn forced him to buy the Irish MPs by giving them a Home Rule bill, which further angered the Tories and their Ulster Protestant allies, who threatened violence and began to arm themselves.

Churchill, by nature an activist and a partisan, if not exactly belligerent, was in the thick of all those struggles. Trade unionists now hated him. Suffragettes, who made him a particular target, tried to break up his meetings and occasionally assaulted him. He was made the victim of a rare physical assault in the Commons. On November 13, 1912, during an Ulster debate, the ultra-Tories shouted "Rats!" to him and Colonel Seely, sitting on the front bench. Churchill characteristically responded by waving a handkerchief, a gesture of irony interpreted as provocation, and Ronald McNeill, an Ulster MP, responded in turn by seizing the Speaker's leather-bound copy of Standing Orders, hurling it in a vast parabola through the tense air, and striking Churchill on the head. He responded by quoting Hazlitt: "I do not mind a physical blow. It is hostile ideas which hurt me." Later he insisted on fulfilling a speaking engagement in Belfast's Unionist Hall, despite threats to his life. This was one of many instances at the time which testify to his lack of physical fear.

In this sense there has never been a more courageous politician. He courted danger, given the chance.

Not that Churchill enjoyed divisions in society—quite the contrary. He found the center attractive. He and Lloyd George discussed the possibility of a new party of all talents. In his case it was made more attractive by his friendship with the Tory MP F. E. Smith. Son of a former mayor of Birkenhead and prizewinning lawyer from Wadham College, Oxford, "F. E.," as he was known, had made in February 1906 what is rated the greatest of all maiden speeches and had almost immediately taken a prominent place on the Conservative front bench. He and Churchill soon became fast friends. Smith made a tremendous income at the bar and helped Churchill in a libel action. He was witty, abrasive, profane, a great hater and enthusiast, the only person Churchill admitted had a finer brain than himself. They argued, drank, and joked together into the night, and Clemmie believed he was the worst possible influence on her husband, more even than Lloyd George, who at any rate had the (to her) merit of going to bed at nine if he could. Smith was the only friend with whom Churchill watched his words, for he feared that Smith, who was the master of insults, might if they quarreled use expressions which would end their friendship forever. To Clemmie's horror he was asked to be Randolph's godfather, and agreed. Churchill thought him a natural for a center party of brilliant individuals. This friendship continued, even intensified, over the budget crisis, the House of Lords crisis, and the Ulster crisis. The only thing they agreed about was denying votes to women, for Smith, who adored them—"he spared no man with his wit, and all women"—and would not allow his daughters to go to boarding school or university, thought participation in public life would destroy femininity. The two men were famous for laughing loud and long together. Unable to dominate as they wished the old-style Literary Club, or "the Club," originally founded by Dr. Johnson, they created a rival, "the Other Club," which they stocked with their friends, and which became even more famous for scintillating talk and vitality, if not for wisdom. It was a bridge between two hostile worlds, as Tories shut their doors in Liberal faces. It was one of the rare times in English history when members of the two parties did not meet at dinner or in ballrooms. New York and Paris were used to bitter political schisms, but London had always put social relations before party, and the bitterness was painful as well as novel. Smith joked: "We have got the best of the bargain. We are sought out by duchesses. Countesses give dinner parties for us. What do you Liberals get? The Society of Knights' Ladies."

Actually there is no evidence Churchill was ever excluded by the Mayfair hostesses as a result of his views, or for any other reason. They were delighted to have him, then as always. In any case he had resources of his own. He and Clemmie had always contrived to be "well-mounted," a horsey term which he used to signify "able to maintain a comfortable existence in society." As he once put it: "All my life, I have earned my own living, so that I have always had a bottle of champagne for myself and another for a friend." In 1911 Asquith, hearing the rumbles of war grow louder, transferred Churchill to the Admiralty. As first lord, he became "tenant of the grandest tied cottage in Whitehall," as he put it. At Admiralty House his retinue of indoor servants expanded from seven to twelve, and Clemmie was able to preside over sumptuous dinner parties and receptions. Nor was this all. He had the use of the Admiralty yacht, the *Enchantress,* at four thousand tons one of the largest afloat, with a crew of 196. He delighted in this splendid vessel: "It was the finest toy I ever had in my life." Luxury yachting under blue skies was the greatest pleasure of the prewar ruling class. He provided it in regular spring and summer cruises on the grand scale for his social and political friends, from the Asquiths down. There are rapturous accounts of these occasions. There was nothing frivolous about them, however. The Royal Navy was the most complex and widely spread fighting machine on earth. It was "the Senior Service," dogmatically proud of its ways and determined not to change them. The senior admirals regarded Churchill with horror. Junior officers, petty officers, and ratings saw him as a hero, especially after he improved their pay and conditions. There were many hundreds of naval establishments and bases in the British Isles and the Mediterranean alone. Thanks to *Enchantress,* Churchill visited every one of them, spending eighteen months on board her during his three peacetime years as first lord. He looked into everything and everyone. He often worked eighteen hours a day, and absorbed the new technology of naval warfare with impressive speed. It was exactly the kind of existence he loved. Against frenzied opposition he created a naval staff. He began the historic switch from coal to oil, and in the process laid down a new class, the Queen Elizabeth, of huge, oil-burning battleships. He created the naval air service, and begged his ship architects to design him aircraft carriers. He learned to fly himself and did so, with reckless delight, as often as he could, until Clemmie, on her knees, persuaded him to give it up. He recognized no limitations to his activities and took the government, and

Britain, into the oil industry by investing in Persia and creating the great Anglo-Persian Oil Company (now BP). This proved to be, over the decades, an even better investment than Disraeli's purchase of the Suez Canal.

Surveying the world scene from his coign of vantage at the Admiralty, now, thanks to his efforts, in direct wireless communication with every part of the world, Churchill sensed that Britain was heading for a war with Germany. While still home secretary he judged it his duty, as the minister responsible for international security, to attend German army maneuvers. The kaiser, who was part English and spoke the language fluently, made a fuss of him and Churchill got to know him quite well, insofar as anyone did. For the kaiser, as Churchill made clear in an essay in *Great Contemporaries* (1937), was an enigma and a mass of contradictions. It was unclear whether he was a puppet or an autocrat. What was undeniable, as Churchill saw for himself, was that Germany possessed the best professional army in the world. He attended French maneuvers, too, and, despite his lifelong Francophilia, he could see there was no comparison. Moreover, Germany was now easily the largest industrial power in Europe and, with a large and rapidly growing population, capable of expanding her war machine dramatically. On his return from German maneuvers, Churchill said, "I can only thank God that there is a sea between England and Germany."

The sea was defended by the Royal Navy, the largest in the world, though no longer up to the "two-power standard," able to take on and defeat the two next largest navies in the world. That raised the question: why were the Germans, with an army capable of domination of all Europe, determined to match, or at least challenge, Britain at sea? Their navy could only be aimed at Britain and the global command of the sea. The Germans began building their High Seas Fleet, as they called it, in the late 1880s, and continued to increase the rate of ship construction, especially of armored, big-gun battleships, over the next twenty years. It was this plainly anti-British construction program which turned public opinion, hitherto pro-German, if anything, against what were now referred to as "the Huns." (Churchill preferred the French term of abuse, *boche*.) When Churchill took over the Admiralty, the policy was then to maintain a 60 percent superiority over Germany in modern battleships. But this was upset by the German Naval Law of 1912 which increased their battleship construction rate by half again. Churchill responded with the Queen Elizabeth class, the largest warships ever made at 27,500 tons and eight fifteen-inch guns each, oil burning and able to maintain high speeds. A disgusted Lloyd George complained that Churchill had lost all interest in social reform "and now talks about nothing but boilers."

Churchill was also concerned by the German decision to build large numbers of U-boats (as they called them). What were they for? The answer was unmistakable. Britain had the largest merchant navy in the world and imported a greater percentage of her food than any other great power. The German U-boat was a potential war-winning weapon which could starve Britain to death. Churchill began to hate the U-boat passionately, and near the end of his life he declared that in both world wars the submarine threat had worried him more than any other. The only answer was to build large numbers of U-boat destroyers, or destroyers for short, very fast and equipped with a new weapon, the depth charge. This he did. But at every step in his policies, he was opposed by elderly admirals, of whom there were a large number occupying key positions. He spent as much time battling with them as he did at the actual work of modernizing the navy.

It says a lot for Churchill's overwhelming energy that while performing all his myriad tasks at the Admiralty and the naval bases, he did many other things, too. He stood by Lloyd George in his many troubles—accusations of corruption over Marconi shares, and of fornication and adultery—and backed Asquith to the hilt over Home Rule. There was much gunrunning among both Protestants and Catholics and threats by Ulster Protestant army officers, many of whom held senior posts, to resign their commissions rather than participate in coercing Ulster to accept Home Rule. He made two hazardous visits to Ulster, on one taking Clemmie, to put the government's case, and he was prepared to use force to ensure that Ulster abide by the Home Rule compromise. It is worth noting that in the years 1911–14, Churchill felt bound to pursue policies which antagonized most of the senior admirals and many of the senior generals. This helps to explain his troubles during the war. Indeed, though he was not at all an extremist, his actions often looked extreme. His nature was such that, once a policy was finally determined in the cabinet, he pushed it with enthusiasm bordering on recklessness. Ulster was determined to fight, as his father had said. He himself now believed that London should fight, and would be right—though he never actually said it. But in a speech at Bradford on March 14, 1914, he said that it was time to "go forward together and put these grave matters to the proof." He ordered the Third Battle Squadron to be within an hour's sailing from Belfast, to show that the legitimate government was serious about using force. Fortunately Asquith quickly canceled the order. But it was known, and bitterly resented, that Churchill was the foremost in the cabinet in his willingness to coerce Ulstermen, whose greatest pride was that they were "loyalists" and stuck by the empire, unlike the southern Irish Catholics who were violently anti-British. If Churchill found himself uncomfortable in this unusual role he did not show it. He put himself firmly on the side of parliamentary institutions and the rule of law. And, as always, action for him was more heartening— and delicious—than sitting behind a constitutional desk. If the crisis had exploded into civil war, as looked likely by July 1914, it is not clear what Churchill would have done. But the coming of European war shoved Ulster violently onto the back burner, and Churchill eagerly turned his attention in a totally different direction.

In fact he had been working for some months to get the navy into a high state of readiness, and as the buildup to war accelerated, he ordered the navy not to disband after its summer maneuvers but to take up action stations. From the start of the crisis, he was a prominent member of the war party. The issue to him was Belgium and her ports, especially Antwerp. Britain had always been opposed to these ports, aimed like pistols at her coast, being in the hands of a major power, especially France. That was why Britain gave a solemn guarantee of Belgian independence. Now Germany was the threat, and when the right wing of the German army, as part of the "Schlieffen Plan" to subdue France, swung through Belgian territory, Churchill was enthusiastically in favor of Britain sticking to the guarantee—"a mere scrap of paper" as the kaiser bitterly called it. Moreover he persuaded Lloyd George to take the same view and thus prevented the breakup of the government, though he was unable to stop Lord Morley, his friend and mentor, from resigning. When war came Churchill was ready, prepared psychologically and in every way, for what he realized would be the biggest conflict in history. He was like a man who had long schooled himself for a job and was now told to do it. And he had got the vast machine for which he was responsible geared up, too. The war, in many ways, proved a disaster for Churchill. But on his downfall, Lord Kitchener, who had been made chief warlord at the outset, reassured him, "There is one thing, at least, they can never take away from you—when the war began you had the fleet ready."

Chapter Three

The Lessons of Failure

Though Churchill entered the Great War readily, if not eagerly, we must remember that he had warned in speech and print that it would be a catastrophe for humanity. He was the only one, apart from that brilliant prophet of the future H. G. Wells, to predict its horrors so clearly. And they proved worse than either supposed. Indeed the first of the two world wars proved the worst disaster in modern history, perhaps in all history, from which most of the subsequent problems of the twentieth century sprang, and many of which continue, fortissimo, into the twenty-first. He saw all these tremendous events from a highly personal viewpoint and portrayed them vividly, seen from close quarters and invested with strong emotion. As with every major event in his life, he told the story as soon as it was over, on an appropriately large scale. A. J. Balfour, who always viewed him with a salty mixture of admiration and vitriol, put it: "Winston has written an enormous book about himself and called it *The World Crisis.*"

Even before the book appeared, he had epitomized its monstrous nature in glowing words on a sheet of War Office paper:

All the horrors of all the ages were brought together, and not only armies but whole populations were thrust into the midst of them. The mighty educated states involved conceived—

not without reason—that their very existence was at stake. Neither peoples nor rulers drew the line at any deed which they thought could help them to win. Germany, having let Hell loose, kept well in the van of terror; but she was followed step by step by the desperate and ultimately avenging nations she had assailed. Every outrage against humanity and international law was repaid by reprisals—often on a greater scale and of longer duration. No truce or parley mitigated the strife of the armies. The wounded died between the lines: the dead mouldered into the soil. Merchant ships and neutral ships and hospital ships were sunk on the seas, and all on board left to their fate, or killed as they swam. Every effort was made to starve whole nations into submission, without regard to age or sex. Cities and monuments were smashed by artillery. Bombs from the air were cast down indiscriminately. Poison gas in many forms stifled or seared the soldiers. Liquid fire was projected upon their bodies. Men fell from the air in flames, or were smothered often slowly in the dark recesses of the sea. The fighting strength of armies was limited only by the manhood of their countries. Europe and large parts of Asia or Africa became one vast battlefield on which not only armies but entire nations broke and ran. When all was over, torture and cannibalism were the only two expedients that the civilised, scientific Christian states had been able to deny themselves, and they were of doubtful utility.

At the time, Churchill was too busy to reflect on the horrors of war. He was responsible for 1,100 warships, with more joining them every week from the shipyards. But they were vulnerable. Three cruisers were lost to a U-boat on a single day, September 22, 1914. In October the battleship *Audacious* was sunk and soon after two more cruisers went down in the lost battle of Coronel. Combined loss of life was over four thousand. The failure of the Mediterranean fleet to sink two German warships on their way to Istanbul inspired Turkey to join the war on Germany's side. On two occasions German warships made hit-and-run attacks on Yorkshire towns. The fact that the navy had enabled the six divisions of Britain's expeditionary force to be transported without loss of a single man was taken for granted, though it was a notable achievement. Churchill sent fast battle cruisers to the South Atlantic to avenge Coronel, and they did so at the battle of the Falklands, the entire German squadron being sent to the bottom. But that was taken for granted, too. The public demanded to know what the Grand Fleet was doing, and why it had not won an overwhelming victory. Why had there been no Trafalgar? Where was Nelson? The French had saved Paris by their victory at the Marne in early September, but Britain had made no spectacular contribution as yet to victory in the war, which all (except Churchill and Kitchener) believed would be short.

In his frustration, Churchill involved himself in a typical personal adventure. He had already created a naval division for land use and set up a base in Dunkirk, with a naval air squadron, and commandeered Rolls-Royces protected by sheets of steel armor, the earliest version of the tank. When news reached the cabinet that the Belgians were about to surrender Ostend and Antwerp, thus defeating the whole object of Britain's intervention in the war, it ordered Churchill, a delighted volunteer, to go to Antwerp to take charge. He did so and had a tremendous time, commanding every available man and piece of artillery, improvising, and inventing new weapons. He afterward described it in *The World Crisis* with rhetorical relish. He set up his HQ in the best hotel, went around in a cloak and a yachting cap, and held the city for a week, during which the three chief French Channel ports, essential links between Britain and the expeditionary force, were made secure. But his proposal that he resign his office and be appointed commander on the spot, though approved by Kitchener, was rejected by the cabinet, and he was ordered home. Antwerp fell, and with it two thousand British troops who were killed or taken prisoner, and Churchill was blamed, particularly by the Tories and senior army generals. Clemmie, who had had a baby (Sarah) while her husband was fighting, was also critical. But the prime minister was warm in praise: "He is so resourceful and undismayed, two of the qualities I like best."

Churchill later wrote that "the weight of the War" pressed "more heavily" on him in the last months of 1914 than at any other time. As the enormous and constantly expanding armies settled down into static, bloody, and horrible trench warfare in Flanders, Churchill feared his nightmare vision was coming true: the vision of an endless, infinitely costly but indecisive war, in which all would lose, none gain, and the only result would be the ruin of Europe and her empires. The navy had painfully succeeded in bottling up Germany, clearing the seas of her surface ships and maintaining British maritime supremacy on the oceans. Otherwise it was unoccupied and denied the chance to strike a vital blow. Admiral Jellicoe, commanding the Grand Fleet, was rendered cautious, perhaps excessively so, Churchill felt, by his knowledge that though he could not win the war by daring, he could "lose it in an afternoon" by one serious misjudgment. How to restore dynamism to the war? He asked Asquith (December 29, 1914): "Are there not other alternatives than sending out armies to chew barbed wire in Flanders? Furthermore, cannot the power of the Navy be brought more directly to bear upon the enemy?"

One answer was to make more use of Russia's almost inexhaustible manpower resources by shipping vast supplies of modern weapons, especially heavy artillery, to her Black Sea ports. But this meant knocking Turkey out of the war, or at any rate clearing the Dardanelles to let the British and French munitions ships through. This is what Churchill suggested in a memo to Asquith at the end of 1914. He also offered an alternative: an invasion of Schleswig-Holstein, which Germany had conquered from Denmark in Bismarck's day. This, he calculated, would bring Denmark, perhaps all the Scandinavian countries, into the war and also open up communications with Russia. But Churchill preferred an assault on Istanbul, which would be easier, given overwhelming Franco-British superiority in the Mediterranean, and bring the Balkan states of Greece, Rumania, and Bulgaria into the war on the Allied side, probably Italy also.

This view was accepted in principle. But now it became clear, at least in retrospect, that Asquith, as prime minister, did not know how to run a war on such a scale. What British prime minister ever had? Aberdeen had made a gruesome mess of British participation in the Crimean War. Pitt had blundered repeatedly in the Continental War against Revolutionary France and Napoleon. Asquith, over six years, had proved a skillful peacetime leader, steering Britain through several crises by his adroit management of the House of

Commons and the cabinet. But he had no conception of the right way to win a world war. He could keep the cabinet together and see that general policy orders were given to the services. But then he sat back and wrote amorous letters to his beloved Venetia Stanley or played bridge endlessly at his house, the Wharf. It is clear now that he should have handed over to a younger and more energetic colleague such as Lloyd George, or formed a war cabinet to conduct the actual operations and the mobilization of the economy. He should also have brought the other parties into the government and so united the nation. But he was not willing to do any of those things.

Hence the attempt to seize the Dardanelles, the narrow strip which was the key to the Sea of Marmara and Istanbul, was a disaster. The year before, Churchill had foolishly brought out of retirement Admiral Sir John Fisher, the dynamic force—he was more than a human being—who had created the original Dreadnought and two more classes of capital ships, to replace Admiral Louis Battenberg, forced out by popular prejudice because he was of German blood, as first sea lord. Fisher was now well into his seventies and increasingly arbitrary and childish (his wild letters often ended "Yours till Hell freezes"). He could not make up his mind about the Dardanelles and in the end opposed it. By this time, January 1915, the Germans and Turks had got wind of the scheme and were preparing to kill it on the beaches. There was a foolish tendency, not shared by Churchill, to underrate the Turks as fighting men. With a large contingent of German officers to advise and train them, the Turkish army was formidable. On January 31, Asquith told Fisher, "I have heard Mr. Winston Churchill and I have heard you and now I am going to give my decision . . . The Dardanelles will go ahead."

If Asquith had then appointed Churchill supremo of the operation (and told him to replace Fisher), the campaign might still have succeeded. But he did no such thing. He was already thinking of forming a coalition with the Tories and knew they would require Churchill's departure from the Admiralty as part of the price. There were endless arguments about the nature of the naval force and the relative importance of the army in the attack. The admirals were timid. The land commander, General Sir Ian Hamilton, was charming but lacked resolution. There were leaks from the cabinet, which under Asquith had no sense of the absolute need for security, and by the time the operation began at the end of April 1915, the assaulting troops, mainly Australians and New Zealanders, plus Churchill's naval division, had not a chance. It was a massacre, and the casualties enormous. The divided command insisted on reinforcing failure, thus breaking the most elementary rule of strategy, and the death toll rose. Fisher noisily resigned, and Asquith formed his coalition, moving Churchill, despite his almost tearful protests, from the Admiralty to the nonjob of chancellor of the Duchy of Lancaster. It was the only time in his life that Clemmie Churchill made a dramatic appeal on behalf of her husband. She wrote to Asquith: "Winston may in your eyes, and in those with whom he had to work, have faults, but he had the supreme quality which I venture to say very few of your present or future Cabinet possess—the power, the imagination, the deadliness, to fight Germany." This was true but unavailing: Asquith was beginning to fight for his own political survival and he saw that the sacrifice of Churchill was essential to it. Besides, his noisy and dominating wife, Margot, whose shouted advice was to get rid of Churchill at any cost, told him: "I have never varied in my opinion of Winston I am glad to say. He is a hound of the lowest sort of political honour, a fool of the lowest judgment, and contemptible. He cured me of oratory in the House, and bored me with oratory in the Home."

So Churchill was out and had to watch, impotent and silent, while the politicians, admirals, and generals compounded their mistakes and the operation, after a quarter of a million casualties, ended in ignominious evacuation. Though an official inquiry eventually exonerated him, at the time (which is what mattered) he got the blame. As Theodore Roosevelt once remarked of a financial crisis: "When people have lost their money, they strike out unthinkingly, like a wounded snake, at whoever is most prominent in the line of vision." Here it was not money but lives lost, and there was no doubt who was most prominent. So the Dardanelles disaster became identified with Churchill and the fury this aroused persisted until 1940, and even beyond, especially among the Tories and a huge chunk of the public.

It was the lowest time in Churchill's life. At this point, Sir William Orpen, Britain's finest painter, did his portrait. It is the best ever done of Churchill, of the fifty or so that have survived, and one of the best Orpen himself ever produced: dark, somber, troubled, defiant—just—but more despairing. When it was finished, Churchill sighed, "It is not the picture of a man. It is the picture of man's soul." Orpen used to speak of "the misery in his face." He called Churchill "the man of misery." No one can understand him properly without looking long and earnestly at this great work (now in Dublin). A quarter of a century later, when Churchill was back at the top and able to look at his life more philosophically, he said, "Yes, it's good.

He painted it just after I'd had to withdraw our forces from the Dardanelles, and I'd got turfed out. In fact when he painted it I'd pretty well lost everything." He brooded in his inactivity, something he had never experienced before. His wife later told Martin Gilbert, his great biographer, "I thought he would die of grief."

At this moment, providence intervened. By pure chance, his sister-in-law "Goonie" Churchill (Lady Gwendeline Bertie, daughter of the Earl of Abingdon) was painting in watercolor in the garden of Hoe Farm in Surrey, which they had rented jointly. Churchill: "I would like to do that." She lent him her paints and soon, ambitious as always, he sent for a set of oils and canvases. He loved it. The Scots-Irish master Sir John Lavery, a neighbor, took him in hand, and his dashing wife, Hazel, also a painter, gave him excellent advice. "Don't hesitate. Dash straight at it. Pile on the paint. Have a go!" He did, with growing relish. He discovered, as other sensible people have done, that painting is not only the best of hobbies but a sure refuge in time of trouble, for while you are painting you can think of nothing else. His first painting, *The Garden at Hoe Farm*, with Goonie in the foreground, survives. Soon, misery began to retreat. His mind, his self-respect, his confidence were restored. He found he could paint strikingly and loved it; his efforts improved with each canvas. The colors were strong and cheerful. His friends liked them and were delighted to have them. He had discovered a new field to conquer with his audacity. Painting, after politics and the family, became his chief passion, and he painted for the rest of his life, as the perfect relaxation from his tremendous cares. His eventual election as an Honorary Royal Academician Extraordinary in 1948 may have been colored by his wartime eminence. But it is a compelling fact that in 1925 Lord Duveen, the leading art dealer of the century, Kenneth Clark, later director of the National Gallery, and Oswald Birley, one of the top portrait painters, formed a committee to award a prize to works of art submitted anonymously by amateur artists. The three gave it instantly and unanimously to Churchill's submission, *Winter Sunshine,* and Duveen found it hard to believe the painter was an amateur.

Enlivened by art, Churchill determined to go back into the fray by fighting in Flanders. He went to the front on November 18, 1915, and was there till May 1916. After much opposition, he was given a battalion to command, the Sixth Royal Scots Fusiliers, and saw action in the trenches. A photograph survives showing him wearing a French infantryman's helmet, which he preferred to the British tin hat, and dressed in a uniform so badly put on and buckled as to cause heart failure in Sir Douglas Haig, the ultrasmart commander in chief, who as Lloyd George scathingly put it, was "brilliant to the top of his boots." But he looks happy. The experience restored his faith in himself and winning the war. He later wrote:

As, in the shadows of a November evening, I for the first time led [my men] across the sopping fields which gave access to our trenches, while here and there the bright flashes of the guns or the occasional whistle of a random bullet accompanied our path, the conviction came into my mind with absolute assurance that the simple soldiers, and their regimental officers, armed with their cause, would by their virtues in the end retrieve the mistakes and ignorances of staffs and cabinets, of admirals, generals and politicians—including, no doubt, many of my own. But alas at what a needless cost! To how many slaughters, through what endless months of fortitude and privation, would these men, themselves already the survivors of many a bloody day, be made to plod before victory was won!

Churchill's service in the trenches served him well in both world wars because it enabled him to understand the views of ordinary soldiers and officers (much better than Sir Douglas Haig, who never went near the trenches if he could help it: he thought his nature too tender and that experiencing horrors would undermine his ability to take hard decisions). He returned to London exhilarated, eager for work—and to earn money to replace his ministerial salary writing articles for the *Sunday Pictorial* and the *Times*.

After demeaning attempts to cling on, Asquith was finally ousted in December 1916 and replaced by Lloyd George, who began to do many of the things that should have been automatic from the beginning of the war. He wanted to bring Churchill back, but the Tories in his coalition would not hear of it. After a key meeting with LG behind the Speaker's Chair in May 1917, Churchill became his unofficial adviser on the war, though holding no office. Thus "master and servant" were reunited and Churchill, chastened by his experiences and aware of the risks the prime minister was taking to talk to him at all, was for a time silent and almost servile. His position, however, was helped by his alliance with a new friend, Max Aitken, Lord Beaverbrook, a Canadian financier who was rapidly building up one of the most successful newspaper empires in Britain. They became intimate friends and the Beaverbrook press sang his praises.

Clemmie disliked him even more than she did F. E. Smith, and thought his advice to her husband always wrong and often inflammatory. In my experience of Beaverbrook I found him shrewd and often wise, honest, reliable, and truthful. But many thought otherwise and agreed with Clemmie. At all events, by July 1917 Lloyd George felt strong enough to bring back Churchill and made him minister of munitions.

This was a brilliant move, and Churchill rapidly made himself one of the most efficient departmental ministers in British history. It was a confused ministry which had grown up haphazardly during the war and was a maze of duplications, contradictions, and bureaucratic gang warfare. In a short time of fanatical hard work Churchill made it simple, logical, and efficient. He forged a close link with the front to ensure the troops got exactly the right weapons and ammunition they wanted, in the right quantities. He visited the front constantly, and Haig was so impressed by the improvement in supplies that he completely reversed his opinion of Churchill and let him use the Château Verchocq near Calais. Within a year, the British army was better supplied with weapons of their choice than either the French or the Germans. The vast quantities of heavy artillery, mobile cannon, and machine guns Churchill sent played a notable part in the slaughter inflicted on the German divisions, which attacked in March 1918, when for the first time in the war the relative casualty rate was decisively reversed. The German army began to bleed to death—the prime cause of their plea for an armistice in November 1918. Churchill was also effective in ensuring that American forces, arriving at the front in growing numbers from late 1917, never went short of munitions. There is a vignette of Churchill, after a day at the front, getting lost in his Rolls-Royce near Verchocq and shouting to his driver, "Well, it's the most absolutely fucking thing in the whole of my life." It is worth noting that Churchill, who disliked swearing in others and usually restrained himself, occasionally indulged when things went wrong. His secretary Elizabeth Layton once recorded: "He was in a very bad temper all this week, and every time I went to him he used a new and worse swear word."

Lloyd George also used Churchill in various key roles in the creation of a unified command with France in 1918. It was at his suggestion that the prime minister brought General Smuts into the war cabinet, in recognition of the enormous efforts the commonwealth had made to help Britain in the war. Soon after the armistice, LG held a general election, which he won with a huge majority for his coalition, Churchill defending Dundee again, as a Liberal (coalition). LG now felt strong enough to make full use of Churchill, bringing him into the cabinet and putting him in charge of both the army and the air force. His first job was to get the soldiers and sailors home as quickly as possible, and this he did with a brilliant scheme, entirely his own, whereby priorities were decided simply by length of service, wounds, and age. As he put it, "I let three out of four go and paid the fourth double to finish the job." This worked, as did a surprisingly high proportion of his ideas. It would be hard to say whether he produced, in his lifetime, more superb ideas or phrases.

His ideas, when they prospered, sometimes had a huge effect on the future. When they foundered, they left a desolating feeling of what might have been. He regarded Lenin's Bolshevik coup of November 1917, his subsequent murder of the czar and his family, and the creation of a Communist state as one of the great crimes of history. He was determined to reverse it and sent troops and armies to Russia through Archangel. This intervention had begun before Churchill took over the War Office but he increased its scale and inflated it with his rhetoric, and had he been allowed he would have done more, and for longer. It did not seem to be working, and his colleagues insisted he pull out. Once again, he was "conspicuous," and got all the blame. In a sense it was another Dardanelles. If it had succeeded, more than 20 million Russian lives would have been saved from starvation, murder, and death in the gulag. It is most unlikely that, with Bolshevism crushed, Mussolini could have come to power in Italy, or still less, Hitler in Germany. Imagine the postwar world without either triumphant Communism or aggressive Fascism!

Churchill was never allowed by his critics to forget his failed attempt to extinguish Communism, but he did not pine himself. He had too much to do, especially in the Arab world, where he was much more successful, and his work had immense consequence, and still does. Throughout the nineteenth century it had usually been British policy to treat Turkey, "the sick man of Europe," gently and to try to keep its crumbling empire together. All that changed when Turkey joined Germany in 1914. Then it became Anglo-French policy to strip Turkey of its Arab provinces and divide the spoils. By the Sykes-Picot Agreement of 1916 France was to get Syria and the Lebanon as protectorates, and Britain the rest. At Munitions, Churchill became involved by speeding guns to the advancing army of General Allenby (whom he regarded as Britain's best general) in Palestine, and by providing rifles with which to arm Arab rebels organized by Colonel T. E. Lawrence, the visionary soldier and adventurer who became one of his close friends. The success of Allenby and Lawrence in December 1917 and the subsequent collapse of Turkey made a tabula rasa of the whole vast area which Churchill now began to call the Middle East, on which Britain—and he himself—could paint the future.

He was aware from his Indian service of the variety of Islam and the ferocious force of its fundamentalist elements. He was fond of saying, "The British Empire is the world's greatest Moslem power," with 80 million in India, which was then undivided, alone. In his two Indian campaigns, and in the Sudan in 1899, he had been fighting fundamentalists. So, essentially, had been Britain in the Persian Gulf since the early nineteenth century. The strongest fundamentalist force in the Arab world was the Wahhabi sect, a confederation of tribes ruled by the Saud family. Britain built up a series of Gulf peoples—in Muscat and Oman, Kuwait, Qatar, and Bahrain—whose moderate views and trading interests made them natural allies—to pen the Saudis in and prevent their piratical dhows from raiding communications with India. Britain also made friends with the Hashemite family, hereditary sharifs of Mecca by direct descent from the time of the Prophet Muhammad.

When Churchill took over, first as head of the army and air force, and from early 1921 the Colonial Office, the idea was to make the Hashemites the pivot of British policy. This was frustrated by the ferocity of the Saudis who, the moment Turkish power collapsed, overran most of the Arabian peninsula, slaughtering their opponents and setting up a kingdom which included the majority of the Gulf coast, already recognized as the world's largest oil reserves. Churchill would have liked to reverse this decision, but war-weary

Britain had no relish for another campaign in the East, and the lesson of the recent failure to reverse history in Russia was too painful, even for him. What he did was to concoct with General Trenchard, head of the air force—which Churchill formed into a separate body—methods of using bombers to control large areas of sparsely populated territory. Churchill's backing for the new RAF was enthusiastic and provident, and by the time he moved to the Colonial Office it was easily the largest air force in the world. He also encouraged the expansion of the British air construction industry which, between the wars, was exceptionally fertile and dynamic, and was to save the country, under his leadership, in 1940.

He now remodeled the Colonial Office to found a new and powerful Middle East department, which in the spring of 1921 organized a high-level conference in Cairo to refashion the area in light of the Saudi triumph. This was one of the highlights of Churchill's career, and it gave him a taste for summit conferences he never lost. It was highly productive. Two new kingdoms were created, Iraq and Transjordan, for the two leading Hashemite princes, Emir Faisal, sharif of Mecca, and Emir Abdullah. The role of the RAF was confirmed and a vast new base in Habbaniya in northern Iraq, still in use by the West, was created. This settlement lasted half a century and would have endured longer but for an unfortunate intervention by the world's largest oil company, Standard Oil. While Britain was using Anglo-Persian and Anglo-Dutch Shell to develop the fields in Persia, Iraq, Kuwait, and elsewhere in the Gulf, Standard formed an alliance with the Saudis to develop fields on their territory, which proved the richest of all. American policy almost inevitably backed Standard, and so the Saudis. Thus the Wahhabi fundamentalists became a great power in the Middle East, immune from attack because of U.S. support and provided with colossal sums of oil royalties with which to undermine the moderates everywhere and the Hashemites in particular.

Churchill was painfully aware of the shadows this cast over the future, but there was little he could do about it at the time. What he could, and did, do was to ensure the continuation of the Jewish experiment in making a National Home in Palestine. To reinforce worldwide Jewish support for the Allies, Britain had issued in 1917 a promise known as the "Balfour Declaration" (he was foreign secretary at the time), under which the government promised "its best endeavours" to help the Jews found their new home there "without prejudice to the existing inhabitants." The declaration, of course, did not exactly envisage the creation of Israel, and it was internally a contradiction. But it had the enthusiastic support of Churchill. His time as a Manchester MP had put him in close touch with a thriving Jewish community. He was always pro-Jewish and became (and remained) pro-Zionist as soon as it became a practical scheme. At Cairo and later he was able to defeat attempts to renege on the declaration and wind up the Jewish National Home in response to Arab pressure. On the contrary, he gave it every support in his power, and when in 1922 the House of Commons showed signs of turning against the whole idea, he made one of his greatest speeches, which swung MPs round into giving the Jews their chance. Without Churchill it is very likely Israel would never have come into existence. It is not given to many men to found, or help preserve, one new state: his score was three.

Churchill was meanwhile playing a key role in the latest phase of the Irish problem. He had been at the front, happily, when the Easter Rebellion broke out in Dublin in 1916 and was not involved in the subsequent hangings. By the end of the war, the Irish Republican Army, under the leadership of Michael Collins, the handsome killer-charmer known as "the Big Fellah," had reduced much of Ireland to anarchy. Lloyd George's first instinct was to pacify it by force, bringing in a special army of ex-soldiers whose uniforms made them known as the Black and Tans, and whose tendency to match the atrocities perpetrated by the rebels with similar reprisals made them hated. The net result was that there was no longer any possibility of coercing Ulster into accepting Home Rule, i.e., inclusion in a Dublin Parliament. The problem was: could the rest of Ireland be persuaded to accept a settlement which left the six counties (of Ulster) under British rule? By 1921 Lloyd George was determined to negotiate a settlement along these lines, and he called in to help him Churchill and his lord chancellor, Birkenhead (as F. E. Smith had become). These three men, plus Collins, eventually reached one. Churchill again proved himself, in negotiation, a moderate by nature, infinitely fertile in imaginative compromises, much helped by Birkenhead's legal genius, and the Anglo-Irish Treaty must be counted another of his positive achievements, albeit shared with the other three in the quadrumvirate. This treaty led to the establishment of the Irish Free State, under which southern Ireland had the right to govern itself but retained allegiance to the Crown and remained part of the empire, Ulster could opt out, and British forces committed to leaving southern Ireland. It did not prevent a brief and bloody civil war in the south, when Eamon De Valera led the extreme nationalists, and Collins (who had told Churchill, "We would never have done anything without you") was murdered. But the treaty did include a provision, on which Churchill insisted, to allow the British navy to maintain antisubmarine bases on the west coast ("the Treaty ports"), and it lasted, in most respects, for half a century, until the next Irish explosion came.

Meanwhile Lloyd George, who had enjoyed heady personal power for over three years, engaged in his own Churchill-type adventure on the Turkish coast, where he tried to come to the rescue of Greek communities against the newly invigorated Turkish state under Kemal Atatürk. LG loved small, fierce nations, among whom he numbered Greece, and he wanted to commit British forces to preserve these Greek pockets. Churchill, for once, was in favor of withdrawal from what he saw was an untenable position. LG broke with him over this issue—their relations had already been strained by the Irish crisis and the Honours scandal, for which LG was responsible and when Churchill gave him no sympathy. In what became known as the Chanak crisis, LG was forced to back down, and that effectively ended his coalition government. The Tories had long been restive under a regime in which they provided most of the votes in Parliament and Lloyd George and his cronies had most of the jobs. On October 19, 1922, at a meeting of the Carlton Club, Stanley Baldwin, a newcomer to high politics, made a persuasive speech in which he accused LG of splitting the Liberal Party and threatening to split the Tories, too. The Tories voted to withdraw from the coalition, LG resigned, Bonar Law formed a Tory government, and a general election followed in November. During the campaign Churchill was in great pain (the photos show it) and was rushed to hospital for an emergency operation: "In the twinkling of an eye, I found myself without an office, without a seat, without a party and without an appendix."

Thus, seven years after the Dardanelles disaster, Churchill was again sent to the bottom. Or rather, it was like a game of snakes and ladders, and he had now gone right down a snake and had to face the task of wearily climbing the ladder again, for the third time in his life. It was not so easy now he was nearing fifty. For one reason or another the orthodox Liberals, under the battered but revengeful Asquithians, the Lloyd George Liberals, Labourites, and the Tories all hated and distrusted him. He now had a long record. Seen in retrospect, in the twenty-first century, it seems a record of astonishing variety, most of it admirable. Seen in 1922, it appeared alarming. Nothing daunted Churchill, determined to get back into the Commons. Without that, nothing was possible. With it, and his astonishing powers of persuasion and sheer oratory, everything was possible. Dundee was hopeless: he had come in fourth in 1922. So in December 1923 he stood for Leicester West, as a Liberal free trader, but was well beaten by Labour. He stood again in March 1924, in Westminster (Abbey) at a by-election. This was the famous independent-minded seat where in the late eighteenth century Charles James Fox had triumphed against all the might of the Crown, with the help of the kisses of Whig duchesses. Churchill had no duchesses, for Consuelo, the rich American lady who had married his cousin, the 9th Duke of Marlborough and who was fond of "Cousin Winston," had been cast off and had married a Frenchman. But he had a new admirer: Brendan Bracken, a mysterious Canadian, who had come from nowhere (many thought, quite wrongly, that he was Churchill's illegitimate son) and was busy becoming a millionaire and a power in city journalism, eventually owning the *Financial Times*. He became Churchill's closest and most faithful aide, and thanks to his efforts the seat was nearly won. But a Tory got in by forty-three votes, and all was to do again.

But one of Churchill's strengths, both as a man and a statesman, was that politics never occupied his whole attention and energies. He had an astonishing range of activities to provide him with relief, exercise, thrills, fun, and, not least, money. By the end of October 1923, he had embarked on his enormous record of the First World War, *The World Crisis,* which appeared in multiple volumes between 1923 and 1927. The serialization had begun in the *Times* in February. Together with its *Aftermath* (1929), it is his best large-scale book, much of it written with a kind of incandescent excitement, verging at times on poetry, rage, and even genius. It vindicated his wartime career, so far as possible, and provided a brilliantly lit guide through the dark and horrific war. It made a great deal of money over the years and more than three quarters of a century later is still in print, and read. Its success opened before Churchill an endless vista of publishers' contracts all over the earth, for anything he cared to produce.

It also justified a new venture: a country house. Hitherto he had borrowed and let several. But he wanted one he could fashion as his own. In 1922 an inheritance of a small estate from an old dowager duchess of Marlborough gave him a chance. He sold the estate and invested the proceeds in buying Chartwell, a house of Elizabethan origin, plus three hundred acres, at Westerham in Kent. It was only twenty-five miles from Parliament and had a magnificent view. He called in Philip Tilden, the fashionable art deco–style architect (the mode of the twenties), who had worked for his friend Philip Sassoon and redone Lloyd George's country house at Churt, to modernize it. But much of the planning and design was Churchill's own work. It had never been a beautiful house, and is not one now (apart from the view). But it is distinctive, personal, and fascinating, an extension of the man himself in brick and mortar, beams and decorations. It has big windows, which Churchill liked: "Light is life," he said. It is equipped for a writer and revolves round the library and study. But it also has an art deco dining room, which saw countless bottles of champagne uncorked, and a dazzling succession of lunches and dinners, conjuring up the age of Lady Colefax and Emerald Cunard, the great hostesses. The real personality of Chartwell, however, lies in the surrounding grounds and buildings, which were entirely of his design and often literally of his creation. As the plaque there states, he built most of the cottage and a large proportion of the kitchen garden wall, having learned to lay bricks in a rough-and-ready manner. He applied for membership in the bricklayers' trade union but was eventually turned down, after much argument—trade union prejudice and Tonypandy playing a part. He excavated mountains of earth in order to create three connected lakes. He had a mechanical digger for this task, of which he became very fond. He treated it like his own prehistoric monster and referred to it as "he." He also laid down railway tracks to speed the operations, first eighteen inches wide, later twenty inches—three in all—and used various devices to insulate the lake bottoms and keep the water in. His youngest child, Mary Soames, later recalled, "My childhood was beset by leaking lakes." He populated the lakes with black swans which sang to one another (unlike the silent white swans), danced minuets, and performed other tricks. There were also cows, pigs, and fowl, sheep and goats, budgerigars and a parrot. He took particular trouble stocking the ponds with freshwater fish, goldfish and exotics, and his greatest pleasure was to feed them and encourage guests to do so. As in India, he collected live butterflies and had a specially designed hut to house them. The little estate thus became a wonderland of creatures and activities, the delight of countless guests, and the source of provender at Hyde Park Gate, a place of constant entertainment. Every Monday, a carful of flowers left Chartwell for the London drawing room, and on Thursday there was another carful of fruit and vegetables for the kitchen.

The Churchill family always lived well. There was a succession of first-class cooks. The cellars were ample. He nearly always drank champagne at mealtimes (as was normal among the richer politicians of his generation). His favorite was Pol Roger. Toward the end of his life he said the 1928 vintage, of which he bought a great quantity, was the best ever bottled. Madame Roger became a friend of his and named a special *cru* after him. In turn, when he formed a racehorse stable, he named a horse after the brand. He had a special room for his cigars, of which the Romeo y Julieta was his chosen Havana. But it is important to realize that, though he was almost invariably seen and photographed with a cigar in his hand, his consumption was not large—never more than twelve a day. He did not inhale. His cigars were constantly going out and being relit rather than smoked. He never used a lighter, always very large, specially made matches, of which he once gave me a specimen. He loved the procedure of cigar smoking more than the smoking itself—one reason he never had any smoke-produced trouble with his lungs. As Beaverbrook said, "He smoked matches and ate cigars." As for his consumption of hard liquor, he never gulped but sipped, slowly and at long intervals. Once aboard the yacht of Aristotle Onassis, the Greek shipping millionaire, he was sitting in the main saloon with his host and Professor Frederick Lindemann (later Lord Cherwell), his personal science adviser, when he suddenly said, "If all the whisky and brandy I have drunk in my life was added up, it would fill this state-room to overflowing." Lindemann: "I don't think so." Onassis: "Let us measure the dimensions of this room and see." Churchill told the professor to get out his slide rule and gave him details of his daily intake of spirits over his lifetime. Lindemann got to work and came up with the answer: the saloon would be filled up to the height of five inches. Churchill was plainly very disappointed.

However, if Churchill lived well, he never had much cash in hand or saw his investments rise to a point when he could feel secure for life, or even for the next year. Chartwell cost £5,000 but he had spent £20,000 on it by the end of the 1920s. His finances rollerskated, and on three occasions he feared he would have to sell the house. Eventually, after the Second World War, the *Daily Telegraph* proprietor bought it and endowed it for the National Trust, to be kept in perpetuity as a memorial to Churchill and his day. It was agreed he could live there for the rest of his life at a nominal rent of £300 a year. It was, and is, handsomely kept up and has become one of the choicest attractions for visitors to Britain from all over the world.

All this was in the future. At the time, Chartwell and all it offered in terms of work and enjoyment blunted the sense of loss his exclusion from high politics inflicted, until the wheel of fortune should turn again. And turn it did! It became clear that his only political future was with the Tories. But how to get back among them? So long as Bonar Law lived, there was no chance. He hated Churchill because of Ulster, distrusted him because of the Dardanelles, and found him an infuriating cabinet colleague. Churchill had a pernicious habit, which did him infinite harm, of overrunning the boundaries between the various government departments and speaking in cabinet—without being invited by the prime minister—on issues which were not his direct concern. Nothing makes a cabinet minister more unpopular, and his interventions were controversial and lengthy. He reduced Curzon to rage and even tears, and caused Bonar Law to lose his temper in cabinet, the only time he did so. He recognized Churchill's abilities but said, "I would rather see them displayed as my opponent than as my colleague." However, in 1923 Bonar Law became mortally ill and resigned, saying he was too sick to advise George V about a successor. The job of adviser went to Balfour. He rejected the favored candidate, Curzon, who would certainly never have offered a top job to Churchill, in favor of Stanley Baldwin. In the meantime, Churchill had been worming his way back into Conservatism. He was helped by Birkenhead and by his father's old friend in Liverpool, Alderman Salvidge. They arranged for Churchill to make a big speech in that city in May 1924. In those days, Churchill often took several whiffs of pure oxygen to "lift" him before a bout of oratory, and he traveled up with two canisters. The speech was a tremendous public success and in it he withdrew his old opposition to duties and in effect dropped his free trade views. This public recantation was humbling to make but it achieved its purpose. In September he was adopted as a "Constitutionalist" candidate in the Epping division of Essex, and at the general election in October he was returned with a massive majority of 9,763. It was now the easiest of moves to ask for the Conservative whip and get it, thus making himself eligible for office. It opened up a new era in his life. For the rest of it, he was now seen as a Tory on the great chessboard of Westminster, and had the ideal seat to keep him there.

Baldwin, who had briefly served as prime minister before a Labour interlude under Ramsay MacDonald, was returned with a handsome majority at the election and was in a generous mood. His most important Tory colleague was Neville Chamberlain, whom he originally intended to make chancellor of the exchequer. But Chamberlain wished to be a reforming minister of health. Baldwin, a fellow Old Harrovian, took the opposite view of Churchill to Bonar Law's: "I would rather have him making private trouble in the Cabinet than public trouble outside it." He said, half joking, "I wish to make a Cabinet of which Harrow can be proud," and had Churchill into Number Ten. Churchill was expecting little, and when Baldwin said, "I want you to be Chancellor," he thought it meant of the Duchy of Lancaster, the nonjob he had held in the dark days of 1915. He was tempted to refuse, when Baldwin added, "Chancellor of the Exchequer, of course." Churchill was transformed. He "lit up like a gigantic light-bulb." In a split second he was transformed into a radiant, joyful prince of politics again, a man at the top of fortune's wheel. He said: "This fulfills my ambition. I still have my father's robes as Chancellor. I shall be proud to serve you in this splendid office."

Chapter Four

Success and Disasters

Delighted with his unexpected return to ample power, Churchill was determined to be on good behavior. He would be an exemplary chancellor. There would be no rash gestures of the kind which destroyed his father, no meddling with the work of other ministers, to which he was so prone, above all no disloyalty to the prime minister, to whom he felt profoundly grateful. He formed the habit, early each morning, of going from his own house, Eleven Downing Street, through the connecting inner door to Number Ten, and having a chat with Baldwin before each began work. They became very close and like-minded and never had a dispute, let alone a quarrel, throughout the ministry (1924–29).

Churchill introduced five budgets, each with a two-hour speech of pellucid clarity, superbly delivered in majestic language—the best by far since Gladstone's golden age and never equaled since. They were immensely popular in Parliament and the country, since they made MPs feel they understood difficult problems of finance and economics, and the population as a whole felt that the man in charge of the national accounts blended prudence and generosity, compassion and common sense, with wit and grandeur. On budget day he always walked from Number Eleven to the Commons, top hat on head, huge overcoat with astrakhan collar, bow tie, his family around him, smiling, waving, exuding self-confidence and prosperity.

His first budget, in 1925, was the most celebrated because in it he not only reduced income tax but also brought Britain back to the gold standard at the prewar parity. No decision in the whole of Churchill's life has been more criticized, then and since. It has been presented as a characteristically rash personal move by an ignorant man who did not trouble to foresee the disastrous consequences. Nothing could be further from the truth. Almost from the moment he received his seals of office—there is a splendid photo of him returning from Buckingham Palace with them, smiling hugely, eyes lit up, the picture of happiness—to April when he announced the change in his budget, Churchill went into the matter with typical thoroughness and enthusiasm. He heard all sides of the case and took the opinion of everyone who had a right to hold one: Montagu Norman, governor of the Bank of England, the great international finance pundit Otto Niemeyer, senior treasury officials past and present like R. G. Hawtrey and Lord Bradbury, academics, and top City men. He had a special lunch with Reginald McKenna, former chancellor and chairman of the Midland Bank, and John Maynard Keynes, the two leading opponents of the gold standard. He received scores of memos and wrote as many. Opponents argued that the gold proposal, especially at a high priority, would make the price of Britain's exports, notably cotton, shipbuilding, steel, and coal, uncompetitive, thus raising unemployment, already dangerously high at over a million. Supporters argued that a strong pound would restore the self-confidence of the City and London's position at the world's financial center and attract capital and investments, thus in the long run creating more jobs. The overwhelming opinion was in favor of gold. Churchill was by nature an expansionist, especially in his private finances, where he never stinted but simply worked harder to pay the bills. But over four months he gradually allowed himself to be persuaded to go for gold.

Keynes attacked him with a famous pamphlet, *The Economic Consequences of Mr Churchill*. After World War II, when Keynesianism became the orthodoxy, Churchill was condemned on all sides and he himself admitted he was wrong. Later still, however, when Thatcherism became the vogue, Churchill was vindicated. By then, of course, he was dead, but the Iron Lady was delighted to come to the aid of his memory: she adored "Winston," as she always called him. We can now see that there is much to be said for the gold standard. It encouraged entrepreneurs to switch from old, low-productivity industries to new ones—electrics, automobiles, aeronautics, high-technology research—and provided the capital to finance such efforts. The kind of advanced industry which came into existence in the thirties, eventually producing the Spitfire and the Lancaster, the jet engine and radar—the new technology which proved so vital in the Second World War—owed a good deal to the gold standard.

At the time, however, there were mixed results. The Tories were pleased, Neville Chamberlain writing to Baldwin: "Looking back over our first session, I think our Chancellor has done very well, all the better because he hasn't been what he was expected to be. He hasn't dominated the Cabinet, though undoubtedly he has influenced it. He hasn't intrigued for the leadership, but he has been a tower of debating strength in the Commons. What a brilliant creature he is!" Birkenhead noted: "Winston's position with the Prime Minister and the Cabinet is very strong." But the effect of high parity soon made itself felt, especially in the coal industry. It had been Britain's biggest and still employed 1,250,000 men. But many of the pits were old, dangerous, and underequipped. The owners, said Birkenhead, were "the most stupid body of men I have ever encountered." In July 1925, claiming that export orders were down as a result of the new higher parity of sterling, they asked the unions to accept a sharp cut in wages—otherwise they would impose a lockout. The unions flatly refused to accept lower wages or improve their productivity. They would turn a lockout into a strike, and with the railwaymen and the transport workers coming out in sympathy, the strike would become general.

For once Churchill was far from belligerent. He was not anti-union at this stage. He had voted for the 1906 act which gave unions exemption from actions for tort (civil damages) despite F.E.'s powerful argument that to create a privileged caste in law was against the Constitution and would, in the end, prove disastrous. Rather than have a general strike, Churchill would prefer to nationalize the mines, or at least the royalties on coal, the government making up any deficit by a subsidy, which he as chancellor would provide. In the meantime he proposed a royal commission to inquire into an agreed solution for the stricken coal industry. "That will at least give us time to prepare," he said. This proved a shrewd move. The prospect of a general strike had been mooted for a generation and inspired terror in many. It was an uncontrolled monster and, once unleashed, where would it end? In a revolutionary socialist government, even a Communist-type regime?

If Churchill had no special animus against the unions, the prospect of Bolshevism in Britain filled him with horror. "Of all the tyrannies in history, the Bolshevik tyranny is the worst," he had said, "the most destructive, the most degrading." They "hop and caper like troops of ferocious baboons amid the ruins of cities and the corpses of their victims." The Russian regime was "an animal form of barbarism," maintained by "bloody and wholesale butcheries and murders, carried out by Chinese-style executions and armoured cars." This was true enough: even under Lenin, there had been 3 million slaughtered. Churchill warned that a soviet in London would mean "the extinction of English civilisation." It was therefore legitimate to do everything to prepare for a general strike, in terms of police and troop plans, emergency supplies, and legal measures. The commission reported in March 1926, accepting his proposal for nationalizing royalties as well as some cuts in wages. The miners, most of whom had already been on strike for a number of months, rejected any cuts: "Not a minute on the hour nor a penny off the pound." Churchill introduced his second budget in April in a stiffening mood. A week later, in May, the general strike began and he took charge of the business of defeating it.

At once he changed back into his earlier activist persona of the Sidney Street siege and the battle of Antwerp. He organized convoys led by armored cars to get food supplies into London. He appealed for volunteers and had a tremendous response from Oxford and Cambridge undergraduates who worked in gangs to replace deliverymen and from young society ladies who operated telephone switchboards. It was class warfare: the upper and middle classes showing class solidarity on the lines of the trade unionists. Above all, Churchill kept up the supply of information to replace the lack of newspapers caused by a printing strike. His original plan had been to commandeer the British Broadcasting Corporation and run a government radio. But Sir John Reith, its director general, flatly refused to let him on the premises and ran a strictly neutral emergency service. So Churchill seized the *Morning Post* presses instead and the reserve supplies of newsprint built up by the press barons, and contrived to produce and distribute a government propaganda sheet called the *British Gazette,* which reached an eventual circulation of 2,250,000. Churchill, having been put in charge of the negotiations, brought about a settlement, which represented a victory for the forces of order. As Evelyn Waugh put it: "It was as though a beast long fabled for its ferocity had emerged for an hour, scented danger and then slunk back into its lair." Churchill had enjoyed himself hugely. His enthusiasm embarrassed his more sophisticated colleagues and evoked jeers and fury from the Labour Party, but in a debate on the strike he dispelled the rancor with a witty and hilarious speech which dissolved the Commons in tempests of laughter. Then he went back to his good behavior: moderation and emollience. But he, with the help of Birkenhead, produced and got passed a Trade Disputes Act which stripped the unions of their more objectionable privileges and held good until 1945, when the Labour Party got an overwhelming majority and, to Churchill's dismay, gave the unions, by statute, virtually everything they wanted.

Churchill's tenure of the exchequer had more serious consequences in a field where he might have been expected to be more sensible: defense. Here he changed his persona completely. From the first lord of the Admiralty who had built up the fleet to over a thousand warships, he reverted to his father's policy of stinginess to the armed services, adding a good deal of rhetoric of his own. He was particularly hard on plans to replace aging warships with new ones such as "silly little cruisers, which would be no use in war anyway." Given his earlier foresight about airpower, he showed no interest in pushing for a class of large aircraft carriers to replace battleships. When in charge of the War Office under LG, he had taken a lead in the government's adoption of the Ten Year Rule, an official assumption there would be no major war in the next ten years, renewed and extended annually. This made exceedingly difficult getting higher spending estimates adopted. It meant Britain emerged from the twenties seriously underarmed for a world power.

What made matters worse was that Japan, hitherto a staunch friend of Britain's, had changed from an ally into a potential enemy. From the 1860s Japan had been transforming itself into a modern power. The Prussians had trained and armed its army and the British its navy, with all its warships being built in British dockyards until the Japanese were taught to design and build their own. The Anglo-Japanese naval treaty, the key to the friendship, came up for renewal in 1922, by which time the Lloyd George coalition was in disarray and had other things to think about. Instead of renewing it, Britain agreed, under pressure from America, which was strongly anti-Japanese, to substitute an international agreement known as the Washington Naval Disarmament Treaty. This laid down a 5:5:3 ratio of capital ships for Britain, the United States, and Japan. The Japanese considered this a condescending insult and never forgave Britain for agreeing to it. There were other irksome provisions—an upper limit of thirty-five thousand tons for capital ships and what the Americans called a "naval holiday." Japan turned nasty and insisted, as part of the agreement, that Britain build no naval bases north of Singapore or west of Hawaii.

Why Churchill did not protest against this antagonism of Japan and the drastic weakening of Britain's naval position in the Pacific, which was to have appalling consequences in 1941–42, is a complete mystery. At this stage of his life he seems to have been completely blind to any danger from Japan. On December 15, 1924, flush with his new office as chancellor and determined on economy, he wrote a letter to Baldwin which used long arguments backed by statistics to show there was no need at all to consider a possible war with Japan:

> I do not believe there is the slightest chance of it in our life-time. The Japanese are our allies. The Pacific is dominated by the Washington Agreement . . . Japan is at the other end of the world. She cannot menace our vital security in any way. She has no reason whatever to come into collision with us . . . war with Japan is not a possibility which any reasonable government need take into account.

Churchill's blindness to the power and intentions of the Japanese extended to the vulnerability of the new base being built in Singapore. Though he frustrated the Labour plan to scrap it altogether, he believed it could be defended mainly by airpower, and it never seems to have occurred to him that the Japanese army could overwhelm it by land, sweeping through Malaya. When this happened, of course, he blamed himself—he never shrank from accepting responsibility when it was just—but it must be admitted he was a prime author of the British debacle in the Far East in 1941–42.

Nevertheless, the twenties were a splendid period in Churchill's life. Baldwin, constantly full of his praise in his letters to the king, called him "the star of the government." The press formed the habit of describing him as "the Smiling Chancellor." His budgets became the "great events of the parliamentary year" (the *Times*). He seemed to Lord Winterton, MP, hitherto a sharp critic, "a man trans-formed . . . head and shoulders above anyone else in the House (not excluding Lloyd George) . . . he has suddenly acquired, quite late in Parliamentary life, an immense fund of tact, patience, good humour and banter on almost all occasions; no one used to 'suffer fools un-gladly' more than Winston, now he is friendly and accessible to ev-eryone, both in the House and in the lobbies, with the result that he has become what he never was before the war, very popular in the House generally."

Everyone tried to have a good time in the twenties. Few suc-ceeded as well as Churchill. He loved bricklaying and excavating, and Chartwell daily grew more beautiful (in his eyes) and "comfy." He painted with increasing skill, having received much detailed ad-vice from the modern master Walter Sickert (who wrote it down and it is well worth reading). He was energetic in play. He kept up his polo until 1927, when he was fifty-three. He hunted, especially wild boar, on the estate his friend Bendor, Duke of Westminster, kept for this purpose in southwest France. He drove a fast motorcar until, in 1925, Clemmie insisted he leave it to the chauffeur. He wrote when possible, completing his Great War volumes and starting work on a grandiose life of his ancestor Marlborough. Bracken arranged highly lucrative contracts. The Churchills lived grandly—he prob-ably consumed more bottles of champagne in the twenties than in any other decade of his life, and there is a vignette of him enjoying 1863 brandy. He had plenty of secretarial help, research assistants and young history dons to advise him. He earned, he spent: it was his philosophy of wealth which he set down in the twenties:

> The process of the creation of new wealth is beneficial to the whole community. The process of squatting on old wealth, though valuable, is a far less lively agent. The great bulk of the wealth of the world is created and consumed every year. We shall never shake ourselves clean from the debts of the past, and break into a definitely larger period, except by the energetic creation of new wealth.

He called for "a premium on effort" and "a penalty on inertia," and he certainly practiced what he preached.

Despite his performance as chancellor, however, the country gave thumbs-down to Baldwin at the general election in 1929. The Tories got more votes than Labour but MacDonald secured the largest number of seats and formed a new government. Ousted, Churchill at once turned to the business of making money on a large scale. In the stock exchange boom of the late twenties he had been prevented from speculating by his position. Now he set to. In America to give highly paid lectures and to write for American magazines, he wrote joyfully to his wife on September 20, 1929, from California that "very great and extraordinary good fortune" had attended him on the stock exchange, thanks to the advice of Sir Harry McGowan, chairman of Imperial Chemicals, whom he had got elected to the Other Club and who, in return, was looking after his money. He instructed Clemmie to embark on plans for large-scale entertainment in London of "colleagues and MPs and a few business people who are of importance." He had earned nearly £20,000 since he last wrote:

> So here we have really recovered in a few weeks a small fortune. And this with the information I can get and now am free to use may earn further profits in the future. I am trying to keep £20,000 fluid for investment and speculation with Vickers da Costa [stockbrokers] and McGowan. This "mass of manoeuvre" is of the utmost importance and must not be frittered away. But apart from this, there is money enough to make us comfortable and well-mounted in London this autumn.

A month later all had gone with the wind as the great Wall Street crash reverberated through the skyscraper canyons. He was present to hear a dinner host address a table full of top businessmen with the words "Friends and *former* millionaires." He added: "Under my window a gentleman cast himself down fifteen storeys and was dashed to pieces." McGowan had been investing his funds "on margin" (something Churchill did not understand), so he not only lost all his money but had to buy himself out of the mess. He considered selling Chartwell, but it was "a bad time." Instead he redoubled his writing output, negotiating fresh contracts and lecture tours. His earnings rose to over £40,000 a year, an immense income in those days. But his confidence had been shaken, and in his bruised condition he began to make political mistakes again.

First he resigned his seat on the Conservative front bench. The issue was India. True, both the new Labour government, plus Baldwin and most of his colleagues, supported by the report of the Simon Commission and the liberal viceroy, Lord Irwin (later Lord Halifax), were united in backing a gradual progression to self-rule. Churchill rejected this totally and got himself into a die-hard position. He fought a campaign, making speeches all over the country, associating with the extreme right-wing of the Tories, and moving closer than ever before to the press barons, especially Beaverbrook and Rothermere, who controlled the *Daily Mail* group. Churchill had not been back to India since 1899. He had only met Gandhi, who now led the resistance movement, once, when undersecretary to the colonies, and mistaking his significance dismissed him as "a half-naked fakir," a phrase which stuck, to his own discredit. His speeches were notably less impressive than those he made as chancellor. Worse, his activities were seen as part of a move to replace Baldwin, in which the press barons enthusiastically joined. This was a huge mistake, for the drive to get rid of him gave "the old turnip lanthorn," as Churchill called him, a new lease on life, and he made some of the best speeches in his career, slaughtering the press lords and putting Churchill right out into the cold. In August 1931 the Labour government collapsed and MacDonald formed a national coalition with Baldwin as number two but the real power, as most of its huge majority were his Tory followers. Churchill was away and does not seem to have been even considered for office. The coalition went to the country and was returned with a vast majority, Labour being reduced to a mere fifty-two seats. Churchill found his majority doubled but he seems, for the moment, to have been without direction in politics, obsessed with the need to make money. So he returned to America to lecture and write.

On December 13, 1931, crossing Fifth Avenue in the dark, he looked the wrong way, as in England, and a fast car, coming from the opposite direction, knocked him down. He was badly damaged on the head, thigh, and ribs, and in terrible pain. But he remained conscious and when a policeman asked what had happened insisted it was entirely his own fault. He was in fact lucky to be alive. A taxi took him to hospital, and he was a long time recovering. He was very down. He told Clemmie: "I have now in the last two years had three very heavy blows. First the loss of all that money in the Crash. Then the loss of my political position in the Conservative Party and now this terrible physical injury." He was afraid he would never recover from these blows. In fact he began the process while still in hospital by dictating a moving and thoughtful article about his accident:

> I certainly suffered every pang, mental and physical, that a
> street accident or, I suppose, a shell wound, can produce.
> None is unendurable. There is neither the time nor the
> strength for self-pity. There is no room for remorse or fears.
> If at any moment in this long series of sensations a grey veil
> deepening into blackness had descended upon the sanctum,
> I should have felt or feared nothing additional.
>
> Nature is merciful and does not try her children, man or
> beast, beyond their compass. It is only when the cruelty of

man intervenes that hellish torments appear. For the rest, live dangerously, take things as they come. Fear naught, all will be well.

He got for this article £600 for world rights, the largest sum he had ever received for a single piece. It was printed everywhere. Then he went back to the fray, shaken but calm, to live more dangerously than ever before, but to fear even less.

Chapter Five

The Unregarded Prophet

Now began the hardest, harshest period of Churchill's life. He was lucky to have a safe seat where he was active, was much loved, and had many faithful friends. Otherwise he might have been extinguished as a politician and become instead a professional writer, for which he had reliable talents. He was lucky to have an adoring (but wise and sometimes critical) wife and a growing family of children who were his warmest supporters. Lucky to have Chartwell, a burgeoning personal paradise where he could lick his many, and often serious, wounds. Lucky to have his art, doing more paintings in this decade (250 out of the 500 that have survived) than in any other. Lucky, above all, that events suddenly gave him a clear vision of what was happening in the world, and what would happen unless he prevented it by his amazing gifts and energies.

The picture cleared early in 1933, when Adolf Hitler captured power in Germany and immediately set about his own plan to destroy Versailles and make Germany the strongest power in Europe, and eventually the world. Churchill had read *Mein Kampf* and believed it represented Hitler's plain intentions. So did Hitler. "My programme from the first was to abolish the Treaty of Versailles . . . I have written it thousands of times. No human being has ever declared or recorded what he wanted more often than me." There was no British response to Hitler's arrival in power. Churchill had already pointed out that the Germans had been breaking the provisions of the Versailles Treaty, which forbade the creation of a large army, for some time, by buying heavy weapons from the Soviet Union. Hitler merely accelerated the process. Few people had read *Mein Kampf;* fewer still believed it. In government circles Hitler was seen as a deluded adventurer who would soon be discarded. The mood of the country was highlighted by a provocative debate at the Oxford Union, in which the undergraduates voted 275–153 for the motion "That this House refuses in any circumstances to fight for King and Country." Churchill called "that abject, squalid, shameless avowal . . . a very disquieting and disgusting symptom." His son, Randolph, now grown up, noisy and attention seeking, often in ways which caused his father acute embarrassment, made a much-publicized attempt to tear the record of the debate out of the Union's book of minutes. Later, Churchill himself calmed down and said, "When it comes to the crunch [a word he invented in this sense] those young men will fight just as their fathers did"—as indeed happened in 1939–45. The future Lord Longford, then a young man, provided a vignette of Churchill in autumn 1935, entertaining young people to lunch at Chartwell. He had spent the morning writing and laying bricks (he told Baldwin he could do two hundred bricks and two thousand words in a day) and was grumpy at first. "But as the wine flowed his eloquence expanded and for three hours the small company were treated to a harangue I have never heard equalled." The theme was German rearmament, and "somewhere around four o'clock, whiskey and sodas were called for and . . . I was emboldened to ask him, 'If the Germans are already as strong as you say, what could we do if they landed here?' 'That should not prove an insoluble conundrum. We are here five able-bodied men. The armoury at our disposal is not perhaps very modern, but none of us would be without a weapon. We should sally forth. I should venture to assume the responsibilities of command. If the worst came to the worst, we should sell our lives dearly. Whatever the outcome, I feel confident we should render a good account of ourselves.' "

Meanwhile, the odds were stacked against his policy: a strong, rearmed Britain, ready and able to oppose a strong, rearmed—and vengeful—Germany. He was deeply depressed about India. He did not see himself as a reactionary longing for a past that was gone, but as the prophet of a dangerous future. The world, he said, was "entering a period when the struggle for self-preservation is going to present itself with great intenseness to thickly populated industrial countries." Britain would soon be "fighting for its life," and the wealth derived from India, the prestige, self-respect, and confidence provided by the Raj, were essential for survival. But India was already going; like China it faced a future of internal chaos, warlordism, and disintegration: "Greedy appetites have already been excited. Many itching fingers are stretching and scratching at the vast pillage of a derelict empire."

But Churchill, pulling out all the stops of his ceaseless rhetoric, failed to rouse the nation, Parliament, or his own party to fight for India. The debate was over giving India an autonomous central government, as well as provincial governments, versus self-government for the provinces only (which Churchill supported). He called the 1935 India Bill, which in effect gave it Home Rule, "a monstrous monument of shame built by pygmies," and he fought it clause by clause. But he never persuaded more than 89 to vote against it, and it passed by the enormous majority of 264. Nor did he have any success, as yet, in alerting public opinion to the dangers of Germany. Keynes had convinced most opinion formers that Versailles was an unjust, destructive, and vicious treaty, "a Carthaginian peace." So Hitler was quite right to seek to undo it. Clifford Allen called it "that wicked treaty" and applauded Hitler: "I am convinced he genuinely desires peace." Archbishop Temple of York said Hitler had made "a great contribution to the secure establishment of peace." Lord Lothian even used the treaty to justify Hitler's persecution of the Jews, which was "largely the reflex of the external persecution to which Germans have been subjected since the war."

It was the only period in British history when pacifism became not merely fashionable but the creed of the majority. In June 1933, at the East Fulham by-election, the Labour candidate received a message from the party leader, George Lansbury: "I would close every recruiting station, disband the army and disarm the Air Force. I would abolish the whole dreadful equipment of war and say to the world, 'Do your worst.' " This was one of six by-elections fought in 1933–34 which registered huge swings in favor of the pacifist candidates. The dominant pacifist wing of the clergy founded a Peace Pledge Union to collect "signatures for peace." A "peace ballot" asked the nation to sign up for a motion repudiating national rearmament and instead to leave everything to the League of Nations. It was adopted by 87 percent of the 10 million votes cast.

At the government level there was no pacifism as such, but folly. One thing Churchill believed in was the French army. He went to its maneuvers and tried to encourage its generals to stand firm against Hitler. But they pointed out that British official policy held the

French army was too big. Sir John Simon, the foreign secretary, told the House that nothing was more likely to provoke a future war than "a well-armed France" facing a disarmed Germany. The same afternoon Hitler's Enabling Bill passed, giving him absolute power to do anything he pleased for an indefinite future. Anthony Eden, for the government, said it was British policy to get the French army cut from 694,000 to 400,000. Churchill protested strongly. Eden rebuked him for opposing measures "to secure for Europe that period of appeasement which is needed." The *Daily Telegraph* noted: "The House was enraged and in an ugly mood—towards Mr Churchill." This was the first sign that he had sacrificed the position of popularity he had so painfully acquired in the twenties by good behavior and was now regarded as a nuisance and a troublemaker. The mood was partly one of disgust with war and horror of a "return to the trenches," and partly fear, especially of war in the air.

Here, Churchill did not help his own cause. In his anxiety to alert people to the danger of Hitler, he voiced the expert consensus that aerial warfare would be devastating. He was well informed, too. In addition to Professor Lindemann, the government allowed him to consult Major Desmond Morton, a specialist in military and economic intelligence. Churchill told the House on November 28, 1934, that up to forty thousand Londoners alone would be killed or injured in the first week of war. Baldwin echoed him: "The man in the street ought to realise there is no power on earth to prevent him [in war] being bombed. The bomber will always get through." General Fuller, the leading expert writer on war, warned that London would become "one vast raving Bedlam," with "the government swept away in an avalanche of terror." Left-wing intellectuals like Bertrand

Russell stepped up the tale of horror: "Fifty gas-bombers, using Lewisite, can poison all London."

To add to Churchill's difficulties, the one issue on which public opinion was roused—the Italian conquest of Abyssinia—had the effect of working against British interests by driving Italy into Hitler's arms. Churchill did not care much about the Abyssinian issue, though he opposed the act of aggression in principle, nor did he see Italy (as Anthony Eden did) as a major threat to peace, more dangerous than Hitler. It was one of Churchill's skills that he could distinguish between levels of power and threat, at any rate in Europe. He thought it was important to keep Italy on Britain's side, as it had been in the Great War, and so keep the Mediterranean firmly under the control of the Royal Navy and the imperial lifeline to India safe. The fuss the government made over Abyssinia, getting the League to impose sanctions (which, of course, did not work), had no effect other than to turn Mussolini into a bitter enemy. He and Hitler signed "the Pact of Steel" and began to coordinate war plans. The Italians had a large fleet and air force, and Churchill realized it would now be necessary to keep half the British fleet in the Mediterranean. He also noted, "The Germans and Italians have 800 bombers between them. We have 47."

On top of it all came the abdication crisis. By 1935 Churchill's campaign to alert the nation was making progress. His speeches were growing more passionate and telling as the danger increased, and more and more influential people were saying to him in public, or more likely in private, that they agreed with him. After a speech on April 23, 1936, giving details of German arms expenditure and Britain's inadequate response, even his old enemy Margot Asquith wrote to him: "I must congratulate you on your *wonderful* speech." She had been lunching with Duff Cooper, soon to become first lord of the Admiralty, Geoffrey Dawson, editor of the *Times,* and other notables: "All were full of praise. It relieved the general depression of all of us, and is terribly *true.* We are at the parting of the ways between war and peace." Churchill was also building up a little group of able MPs in the Commons, such as Harold Macmillan and his old parliamentary private secretary, Robert Boothby. Duff Cooper and Anthony Eden, both in the government, were now with him.

Then the abdication came out of the blue to mesmerize and inflame the nation, to direct attention totally from the external threat, and to show Churchill at his worst. Baldwin said of Churchill, privately, at this time: "When Winston was born lots of fairies swooped down on his cradle with gifts—imagination, eloquence, industry, ability—and then came a fairy who said 'No one person has a right to so many gifts,' picked him up and gave him such a shake and twist that with all these gifts he was denied judgment and wisdom. And that is why while we delight to listen to him in this House we do not take his advice."

This verdict was certainly borne out by Churchill's quixotic support for the worthless Edward VIII in his bid to marry the twice-divorced Wallis Simpson and still keep his crown. Churchill had, as it were, fallen for Edward, a handsome, slim, fragile figure, when he had helped, as home secretary, to install the future king as Prince of Wales at Carnarvon Castle and read out, in a resonant voice, all his many titles of chivalry. He brought out Churchill's childish sense of loyalty and toy-soldier mentality. He went to the support of Edward in the dubious company of Lord Beaverbrook, and much to Clemmie's disgust. As usual he was profuse in offering ingenious solutions for the crisis. But Baldwin, who thought Edward would make a bad constitutional monarch anyway and preferred his brother the Duke of York (the future George VI), outmaneuvered Churchill on every point. In any case, the king preferred abdication to a real battle. As Beaverbrook said to Churchill, "Our cock won't fight, so it's no dice." But when the abdication was more or less inevitable, and MPs were anxious to get it over with and turn to other, pressing matters, Churchill made the error of judgment of a speech urging delay. To his obvious dismay, the House reacted with almost unanimous fury. There were cries of "Drop it" and "Twister," and he was first shouted down by MPs, then ruled out of order by the Speaker. He shouted in fury at Baldwin, "You won't be satisfied until you've broken him, will you," then marched out of the chamber. A few minutes later, almost in tears, he said to another MP: "My political career is finished." Boothby, whom Churchill had not warned of what he intended to do, believed he was drunk after a heavy embassy lunch—the only time when he addressed the House intoxicated—and wrote him a furious letter: "You have reduced the number of your personal supporters to the minimum possible . . . about seven, in all. What happened this afternoon makes me feel that it is almost impossible for those who are more devoted to you personally, to follow you blindly (as they would like to do) in politics. Because they cannot be sure where the Hell they will be landed next." The scene, Lord Winterton wrote, was "one of the angriest manifestations I have ever heard directed against any man in the House of Commons." The *Spectator* summed up the prevailing opinion: "The reputation which he was beginning to shake off of a wayward genius unserviceable in council has settled firmly on his shoulders again."

Without the fall from grace of Churchill in the abdication crisis of 1936, it is possible that the Czech crisis in 1938 might have taken a different turn. Here are two big questions that Churchill asked at the time. The first: if Britain and France had resisted Hitler over Czechoslovakia, would the German generals have overthrown him? Their chief of staff, Field Marshal Ludwig Beck, said to a politician about to visit Britain, "Bring me back certain proof that England will fight if Czechoslovakia is attacked and I will put an end to this regime." But such proof was not forthcoming, and anyway Beck was a cowardly boaster who was soon pushed out without a fight. Baldwin had now retired and Neville Chamberlain, his successor, was even more opposed to war. He actually said in public of Czechoslovakia, the state created by Britain and France at Versailles, along with a "big" Poland and Yugoslavia, to balance German power in Central Europe, "It is a far away country, of which we know nothing." This raises the second question: would the Allies have been better advised to fight over Czechoslovakia in autumn 1938 than over Poland in 1939?

Churchill was quite clear at the time that the answer was yes. The British were now rearming, and Churchill was told that by the end of the year Britain's production of military aircraft would be faster than Germany's. On March 21, 1938, the chiefs of staff presented Chamberlain with a paper, "The Military Implication of German Aggression against Czechoslovakia," which told a terrible story of delays and bottlenecks in the British rearmament program, while admitting it was now gathering pace. The prime minister took from this ambivalent paper the points which backed his view that he must give way to Hitler. Churchill saw the paper and drew the opposite conclusion. His case was this: French morale was beginning to sag and it was vital it should not sag further. It had coordinated its army plans in conjunction with the Poles, Yugoslavs, and above all the Czechs. Germany's claim to the Czech Sudetenland, the essence of the crisis, was designed not to rectify the injustice of Versailles but to knock the Czechs out of the military equation. The Sudetenland included all the elaborate frontier defenses. Without it, Hitler would be able to walk into the rest of the country without a fight—exactly what happened in March 1939. When Hitler occupied Austria in 1938, he not only released four German divisions for service against France but took over six Austrian ones for retraining under the Nazi flag. The Czech business repeated this switch in the military arithmetic on a much bigger scale. Before the Munich surrender in September 1938, the Czechs had forty divisions believed to be the best equipped in Europe. After the swallowing of Prague, the Germans took over the equipment to form forty divisions of their own. So instead of having forty against them they had forty on their side; this switch was equivalent to the entire French army. The Germans also got possession of the Škoda armaments works, one of the largest in the world. Perhaps equally important, there can be no doubt that the French army would have fought with more confidence and effect in 1939 than it did in 1940. All in all, Churchill was right in believing the Munich surrender was of huge military benefit to Hitler.

His speech of October 5, 1938, denouncing Munich was one of his most powerful, and possibly his saddest. What he had to say, he began, was "unpopular and unwelcome." Britain had "sustained a total and unmitigated defeat, and France has suffered even more than we have." The utmost Chamberlain had been able to give for Czechoslovakia "has been that the German dictator, instead of snatching his victuals from the table, has been content to have them served to him course by course." The Czechs would have got better terms by themselves: "Now all is over, silent, mournful, abandoned, broken, Czechoslovakia recedes into the darkness. She has suffered in every respect by her association with the Western democracies and with the League of Nations, of which she has always been an obedient servant." Now that her frontier fortresses were lost "there was nothing to stop the will of the Conqueror." He prophesied that, within months, "the Czechs will be engulfed in the Nazi regime." Churchill added there would be grievous consequences for Britain, for the desertion of the Czechs was the culmination of "five years of eager search for the time of least resistance, five years of uninterrupted retreat of British power, five years of neglect of our air defences." The people were "in the presence of a disaster of the first magnitude which has befallen Great Britain and France . . . All the countries of Central and Eastern Europe will make the best terms they can with the triumphant Nazi Power." Hitler would absorb these regions but "sooner or later he will begin to look westward." This disaster was "only the beginning of the reckoning. This is only the first sip, the first foretaste of a bitter cup which will be proffered to us year by year unless by a supreme recovery of moral health and martial vigour, we arise and take our stand for freedom as in the olden time." This speech rallied the hard core of his supporters, but they were not many. Only thirteen were prepared to vote against the government. So they all agreed to abstain on the motion to approve Munich—thirty of them. For the first time in nearly forty years, his entire political career, Churchill lost his optimism completely. "I am now greatly distressed," he wrote to a Canadian friend, "and for the time being staggered by the situation. Hitherto the peace-loving powers have been definitely stronger than the Dictators, but next year we must expect a different balance."

Then slowly, but with gathering speed, opinion swung against Munich, Chamberlain, and the whole appeasement policy. It was Hitler's actions rather than Churchill's oratory which did it. In January 1939 Hitler took the decision to build an immense fleet of battleships, 3 battle cruisers, 4 aircraft carriers, and no less than 249 submarines. So far as Britain was concerned this was a declaration of war. On March 15 he invaded the remains of Czechoslovakia and annexed them, exactly as Churchill had said. A week later he began to threaten Poland. In April, Mussolini, satisfied that democracy was dead and that "the age of force had arrived," invaded and annexed Albania. In Spain, the military chiefs led by Franco and assisted by Hitler and Mussolini defeated the republican government. Britain and France guaranteed Poland against invasion, and Chamberlain made feeble attempts to draw Russia into a defensive alliance against Hitler. But Hitler easily trumped that and sent his agents to Moscow to sign a pact with Stalin, under which Poland was to be divided between Nazis and Communists, and Russia given a free hand to annex the Baltic states. This was August 1939. The Nazi invasion of Poland followed inevitably on September 1, and Britain and France declared war two days later. Within a month Poland had been swallowed up by the two totalitarian powers.

Since July enormous and puzzling posters had appeared on prominent London sites, asking in giant letters, "What Price Churchill." The man responsible, an advertising agent, later said, "I wanted to get people thinking about the reinstatement of Churchill." In fact it happened swiftly once war was declared. Churchill was invited to accept his old post of first lord of the Admiralty, and he did, together with a seat in a war cabinet of six. He wrote: "A very strong sense of calm came over me, after the intense passions and excitements of the last few days. I felt a serenity of mind and was conscious of a kind of uplifted detachment from human and personal affairs." This was remarkable considering the problems facing him. The year before he had sustained another disaster on the New York Stock Exchange, putting him deeply into debt and forcing him to offer Chartwell up for sale. He was saved by a large and generous interest-free loan from Sir Henry Strakosh, who paid over £18,162.1.10 to Churchill's stockbroker. At the Admiralty he faced countless problems produced by neglect and inertia over many years and by Chamberlain's folly—the Anglo-German Naval Treaty, which Hitler had ignored when it suited him, but which Britain had scrupulously observed, and the agreement Chamberlain had signed with De Valera making the "Treaty ports" no longer available to Britain's anti-U-boat forces.

Despite rumors by his enemies that he was "looking old" and "past it," Churchill worked fanatically hard—out on inspections most days, "Naval Conference" from 9:00 to 11:00 p.m., then dictating late into the night. On September 24 he recorded: "During the last three weeks I have not had a minute to think of anything but my task. They are the longest three weeks I have ever lived." Clemmie wrote: "Winston works night and day. He is well, thank God, and gets tired only if he does not get his 8 hours' sleep—he does not need it at a stretch, but if he does not get that amount in the 24 he gets weary." One of his staff, Kathleen Hill, testified, "When Winston was at the Admiralty the place was buzzing with atmosphere, with electricity. When he was away on tour it was dead, dead, dead." On September 26 he made his first big speech since returning to office. It was a notable success. Harold Nicolson, the parliamentary diarist, recorded: "His delivery was really amazing and he sounded every note from deep preoccupation to flippancy, from resolution to sheer boyishness—one could feel the spirits of the House rising with every word." Five days later he gave an equally successful broadcast to the nation—the first time he used the radio to stir the public. From the blue came a private letter from Franklin D. Roosevelt, offering friendship. Churchill seized eagerly on it to open up a correspondence with the American president which produced over a thousand letters in the next six years and was of incalculable value in bringing Britain and the United States closer, and in transforming U.S. factories and shipyards into workshops for the anti-Nazi crusade.

Hard as Churchill worked, however, he had little power in the general conduct of the war, which languished in inactivity—it was known as "the Phony War"—leaving the initiative to Hitler. In April 1940 the Nazis struck at Denmark and Norway, in May at Holland and Belgium. None put up a fight. The British intervention in Norway was a failure, despite Churchill's efforts. The army proved no good at combined operations, the RAF could not operate so far from its bases, and the Germans controlled the air. German naval losses were heavy: three cruisers and ten destroyers lost, two heavy cruisers and a pocket battleship put out of action. This had the effect later in the summer of helping to dissuade Hitler from a direct invasion of England. On the other hand, in the long term it meant virtually the whole of the western coast of Europe was available for U-boat bases.

It was soon clear that the Norwegian campaign was a disaster, and on May 7–8 the Commons held an impromptu inquest, what became known in history as "the Norway debate." It has been recognized as the most important held in Parliament in the twentieth century. Churchill's speech was the only one made for the government which showed conviction, hope, and resolution for the future. He scrupulously refrained from criticizing his colleagues, especially Chamberlain, even by implication. But it was clear that he was the only minister making sense. Chamberlain was attacked from all sides, one senior Tory quoting Cromwell: "You have sat too long for any good you have been doing. Depart, I say, and let us have done with you. In the name of God, go." Lloyd George said it was the most dramatic climax of a speech he had ever heard. In the vote, the government majority fell from its usual 213 to 81. Many Tories voted against it and there were still more abstentions. Chamberlain decided to resign. It now became obvious there would have to be an all-party coalition. Labour made it clear that it would accept only Halifax or Churchill as leader. Churchill, for once, kept his mouth shut and let others do the talking. King George VI, a conventional man brought up to regard Churchill as a menace, favored Halifax, the establishment candidate. But Halifax ruled himself out: he could not, he said, run a crisis government from the House of Lords. By 6:00 p.m. on Friday, May 10, Churchill got the job he had

worked for. Twelve hours earlier the Germans had begun the decisive campaign against France. Early reports were bad as Churchill
was forming his cabinet. He did not get to bed till 3:00 a.m. But his
courage was high. He recorded:

I was conscious of a profound sense of relief. At last I had
authority to give directions over the whole scene. I felt as if I
were walking with destiny, and that all my past life had been
but a preparation for this hour and for this trial. Ten years in
the political wilderness had freed me from ordinary party
antagonisms. My warnings over the past six years had been
so numerous, so detailed and were now so terribly vindicated, that no one could gainsay me. I could not be reproached
either for making the war or with want of preparation for it. I
thought I knew a good deal about it all and I was sure I would
not fail. Therefore, although impatient for the morning, I
slept soundly and had no need for cheering dreams. Facts
are better than dreams.

Chapter Six

Supreme Power and Frustration

As prime minister and minister of defense, Churchill held power "in ever growing measure," as he himself put it, from May 1940 to July 1945. Probably no statesman in British history had held power for so long in so concentrated and extensive a form. So the first question to ask is: Did Churchill personally save Britain? Was his leadership essential to its survival and eventual victory?

The question is best answered by examining the factors and virtues which operated in his favor—some determined by objective events, others by his own genius and exertions. They were tenfold. First, as a civilian leader, Churchill benefited from a change of national opinion toward the relative trustworthiness of politicians and service leaders—"frocks and brass hats," to use the phrase of his youth. In the First World War, reverence for brass hats and dislike of frocks made it almost impossible for the government, even under Lloyd George at his apotheosis, to conduct the war efficiently. As Churchill put it: "The foolish doctrine was preached to the public through innumerable agencies that generals and admirals must be right on war matters and civilians of all kinds must be wrong—inculcated billionfold by the newspapers under the crudest forms." Lloyd George had the greatest difficulty in sacking any senior figure in uniform and could never take the risk of sacking Haig, the army supremo on the western front, much as he would have liked to.

By World War II, the truth about the mistakes of the brass hats in the earlier conflict had sunk so deeply into the national consciousness that the position had been almost reversed. There was no war hero until Montgomery made himself one late in the conflict by his own victories. Churchill by contrast came to power with the reputation of having been right throughout the thirties, and was now proved right by the danger in which Britain found herself. He never had to hesitate, except for genuine reasons, before sacking a general, even a popular one like Archibald Wavell, the British commander in Egypt. He felt his authority and exercised it: he was seen walking up and down the empty cabinet room once, after a major sacking, saying aloud, "I want them all to feel my power." Churchill was overwhelmingly admired, even loved, but also feared.

Second, the concentration of power in Churchill's person, with the backing of all parties, meant that there were never any practical or constitutional obstacles to the right decisions being taken. He always behaved with absolute propriety. He told the king everything and listened to all he said: within months George VI had swung right round in his favor and wrote, "I could not possibly have a better Prime Minister." He also observed all the cabinet procedural rules. Above all, he treated Parliament, especially the House of Commons, with reverence and made it plain he was merely its servant. These were not mere formulae. Insofar as Churchill had a religion, it was the British constitution, spirit and letter: Parliament was the church in which he worshipped and whose decisions he obeyed. All this balanced and sanctified the huge power he possessed and exercised. Unlike Hitler, he operated from within a structure which represented, and was seen and felt to represent, the nation. He was never a dictator, and the awful example of Hitler was ever present before him to prevent him from ever acting like one. This was particularly important in his relations with his service chiefs, such as General Alanbrooke, Admiral Cunningham, and Air Marshal Portal. He and the cabinet took the decisions about the war. But the way in which they were executed was left to the service chiefs. Churchill might cajole and bully, storm and rant, but in the end he always meticulously stuck to the rule and left the responsible senior chiefs to take the decisions. This was the opposite of Hitler's methods, and one principal reason why he lost the war. In another key respect Churchill did the opposite of Hitler: all his orders, without exception, were in writing and were absolutely clear. When issued verbally they were immediately confirmed in written form. All Hitler's orders were verbal and transmitted by aides: "It is the Führer's wish . . ." Churchill's system of clear written orders, and his punctiliousness in observing the demarcation lines between civilian and military responsibility, is one reason the service chiefs were so loyal to him and his leadership, and indeed revered him, however much his working methods—especially his late hours— might try their patience and bodies.

Third, Churchill was personally fortunate in that he took over at a desperate time. The sheer power of the Nazi war machine, against which he had warned, was now revealed. The worst, as it were, had happened, was happening, or was about to happen. He was able to say in perfect truth, just after he took power (May 13, 1940), "I would say to the House, as I said to those who have joined the government, 'I have nothing to offer but blood, toil, tears and sweat.' " He added, in the same speech, that his aim was quite simple and clear: "Victory at all costs, victory in spite of all terror, victory, however long and hard the road may be; for without victory there is no survival." The last words were of deadly significance, and felt to be so. For Britain was not facing defeat in the sense that it had been defeated in the American War of Independence. It was facing extinction as a free country. Ordinary people were made to feel that. On Churchill's orders, the national anthems of the Allies were played on the BBC before the 9:00 p.m. news every Sunday. There were seven of them, six already defeated, occupied, and under the total control of the Gestapo. Soon, France joined the losers. Churchill certainly did all in his power to save her, paying five perilous visits to consult with her disintegrating, scared, and defeatist government and service chiefs. He would not, however—and rightly—go beyond a certain point. He was prepared to offer France a union of the two states, a most imaginative and adventurous idea, characteristic of his fertility. He was not willing, however, to comply with their request to send all of Britain's precious fighter squadrons to France in a despairing effort to stem the Nazi blitzkrieg. That, he said, would be "hurling snowballs into Hell." Instead, as France lurched toward dishonorable surrender and puppet status under Marshal Pétain, Churchill concentrated on getting the British Expeditionary Force safely back home. And he succeeded. Nine-tenths were rescued from Dunkirk, and many Allied soldiers with them, more than three hundred thousand in all, brought back by an improvised armada of ships, great and small, including pleasure cruisers and fishing boats, which gave picturesque color and even romance to the story, a typically British tale of snatching victory from the jaws of defeat. Thus within a month of taking office, amid the unmitigated catastrophe of France's fall, Churchill was able to report a British victory—Dunkirk—and to speak glowingly of "the Dunkirk spirit." It was in a sense a bogus victory, for the troops had been forced to leave their heavy equipment behind, and in many cases even their rifles, which they had smashed before embarking. But Dunkirk nevertheless gave a huge boost to British morale: now that Churchill was in charge, the people felt that, far from plunging further down into the abyss, the country was moving upward, if only an inch at a time.

Fourth, Churchill himself began to set a personal example of furious and productive activity at Ten Downing Street. He was sixty-five but he looked, seemed—was, indeed—the embodiment of energy. He worked a sixteen-hour day. He sought to make everyone else do likewise. In contrast to lethargic, self-indulgent old Asquith ("the bridge-player at the Wharf," as Churchill called him) or even Lloyd George, who had high tea instead of a proper dinner to discus strategy and went to bed at nine o'clock, Churchill began to wear his own form of labor-saving uniform, a siren suit, easy to put on or take off, in which he could nap if he wanted during long nighttime spells at work. This added hugely to the fast-accumulating Churchill legend: the public called it his "rompers." In fact, thanks to Clemmie, some of these siren suits were of elaborate and costly materials, velvet and silk as well as wool—for "best" parties in the Number Ten bombproof dining room, and so on. Churchill had always used clothes for personal propaganda and had a propensity to collect unusual uniforms. Since 1913 he had been an elder brother of Trinity House, a medieval institution which supervised all lighthouses and port lights in the British Isles. Its uniform had a distinctive nautical flavor and for court dress he always wore it in preference to that of his Privy Council. General de Gaulle, who had by now taken charge of France's resistance forces, asked him what it was and received the mystifying reply, "Je suis un frère aîné de la Sainte Trinité." But the siren suit was the everyday wartime wear and proved a masterstroke of propaganda. In it the prime minister worked within days of taking over, as the first brief and pointed memos and orders flowed out under the famous headline: "Action This Day." So did the endless series of brief, urgent queries: "Pray inform me on one half-sheet of paper, why . . ." Answers had to be given, fast. Churchill had teams of what he called "dictation secretaries." He worked them very long hours. He was sometimes brusque or angry, swore, forgot their names, even lost his temper. But he also smiled, joked, dazzled them with uproarious charm and whimsicalities. They all loved him and were proud to work with him. They helped him to turn Number Ten into a dynamo, and its reverberations gradually resounded through the entire old-fashioned, lazy, obstructive, and cumbersome government machine, until it began to hum, too. Churchill's sheer energy and, not least, his ability to switch it off abruptly when not needed were central keys to his life, and especially his wartime leadership. But it must be admitted that he killed men who could not keep up—Admiral Pound, for instance, and General Sir John Dill—just as Napoleon Bonaparte killed horses under him.

The fifth factor was Churchill's oratory. It is a curious fact that he switched it on to its full power just as Hitler switched his off. Hitler had been, in his time, the greatest rabble-rouser of the twentieth century. In his successful attempt to destroy Versailles and

make Germany a great power again—incidentally ending unemployment—his oratory had been a vital factor in making him the
most popular leader in German history (1933–39). But the Germans, while overwhelmingly behind the campaign against Versailles, had no desire to see Hitler turn Europe into a servile German
empire, let alone lead them into a world war. When Hitler marched
into Prague in March 1939 it was his first unpopular act. Until now
he had ruled mainly by consent. Thereafter it was by force and fear.
Sensing his loss of personal popularity, Hitler ceased to address the
Reichstag or make public speeches. By the time Churchill took
charge, Hitler had retreated into his various military headquarters,
mostly underground, rarely appearing and never speaking in public. He became a troglodyte, while Churchill became a world figure
ubiquitous in newspapers and newsreels wherever Nazi censorship
had no control.

The oratory had two interlocking audiences: the Commons and
the radio listener. Here a personal word is in order. I was twelve
when Churchill took power and had learned to caricature him since
the age of five (I could also do Mussolini, Stalin, and Roosevelt).
My father, having served four years in the trenches and lost friends
in the Dardanelles, was suspicious of Churchill. In April 1940 I re-
call his saying, "There's talk of making that fellow Churchill prime
minister." But by early May events had swung him round: "It looks
as if we'll have to put Winston in charge." By then the nation was
calling him "Winston." My father and I read in the newspaper together all his speeches in the late spring and summer of 1940, and
listened to all his regular broadcasts. The combined effect was elec-
trifying and transforming. I can remember the tone of voice, the

words, many whole phrases to this day. There were two passages in particular. After Dunkirk, and before the last phases in the already lost battle on the Continent, he insisted (June 4):

> We shall not flag or fail. We shall fight in France, we shall fight on the seas and oceans, we shall fight with growing confidence and growing strength in the air, we shall defend our island, whatever the cost may be, we shall fight on the beaches, we shall fight on the landing grounds, we shall fight in the fields and in the streets, we shall fight in the hills. We shall never surrender.

In the Commons, Churchill characteristically supplemented the passage with a joking aside, sotto voce, "We shall fight with pitchforks and broomsticks, it's about all we've bloody got." Jokes were never far away when Churchill spoke, even in the gloomiest times. He was rather like Dr. Johnson's old friend from Pembroke College: "I try to be a philosopher, but cheerfulness keeps breaking in." Of course we did not know that bit about the pitchforks. But the bit about never surrendering rang true. We believed it, we meant it.

After France capitulated, he struck again with memorable words: "Let us therefore brace ourselves to our duty and so bear ourselves that if the British Empire and its Commonwealth last for a thousand years men will still say, 'This was their finest hour.'" People believed this, too, and not only in Britain. Somehow his words were broadcast in Europe, where men and women listened to them at the peril of their lives, and they were believed there, too. At this time, a young archaeology don from Oxford, C. E. Stevens, thought of the V for victory sign. He spent his holidays "pigging it," as he said, with French charcoal burners, and believed they would like it, and so would others. Its Morse code symbols, three dots and a dash, echoed the opening notes of Beethoven's Fifth Symphony. The BBC spread the notion. Churchill adopted it with alacrity and enthusiasm and gave the V sign everywhere with one hand, clutching his huge cigar and holding on to his outsize bowler with the other, as he toured the troops and bombed cities. So the first true victory Britain won in the war was the victory of oratory and symbolism. Churchill was responsible for both.

Sixth, however, came his sense of the importance of airpower and his speed in grasping the opportunities it offered. Under his rule as secretary of state for war and air, just after the First World War, the RAF had been the world's largest air force. It had been grievously neglected in the twenties and early thirties but the level of research and development had been high—Lindemann had explained to him the importance of Robert Watson-Watt in radar and Frank Whittle in advanced jet engines—and by the beginning of the war Britain was producing better aircraft than Germany. By the time Churchill took power, production was equal to Germany's in numbers. He made Beaverbrook his minister for aircraft production and told him to go flat out. By the end of the year British production of war aircraft, both fighters and bombers, had overtaken German in both quantity and quality. So had the output of trained aircrews. Meanwhile, radar stations were spreading all over southern England. For the first time in the war, British technological superiority was established, and Churchill and Beaverbrook put all available resources behind maintaining and lengthening their lead.

The result was that when Hitler and Göring, head of the Luftwaffe, unleashed large-scale air attacks on Britain at the end of June, using air bases in northwest France and Belgium, the RAF was ready and eager. The Luftwaffe's first object was to destroy the RAF's southern airfields. Had this been accomplished there is no doubt that a seaborne invasion would have been launched with a good prospect of establishing a bridgehead in Kent or Sussex. After that the outlook for Britain's survival would have been bleak. But the RAF successfully defended its airfields and inflicted very heavy casualties on the German formations, in a ratio of three to one. Moreover, the German aircrews were mostly killed or captured whereas British crews parachuted to safety. Throughout July and August the advantage moved steadily to Britain, and more aircraft and crews were added each week to lengthen the odds against Germany. By mid-September, the Battle of Britain was won. The sign of defeat was the German decision to switch to night bombing raids on British cities. These caused misery and some loss of civilian life, but the move from hard to soft targets was strategically very welcoming and encouraging for Churchill. As early as August 20 he scented victory and was able to report to the Commons in a speech which contained the memorable tribute to the RAF fighter pilots: "Never in the field of human conflict was so much owed by so many to so few."

Moreover, by now he was able to envisage that the air offered Britain her one big opportunity to move over to the offensive. He wrote to Lord Beaverbrook (July 8, 1940):

When I look round to see how we can win the war I see that there is only one sure path. We have no Continental army which can defeat the enemy military power—the blockade is broken and Hitler has Asia and probably Africa to draw from. Should he be repulsed here or not try invasion, he will recoil eastward, and we have nothing to stop him. But there is one thing that will bring him back and bring him down, and that is an absolutely devastating, exterminating attack by very heavy bombers from this country upon the Nazi homeland.

Churchill knew of course of plans to make an atomic bomb. In the meantime, the Lancaster bomber was being created to carry five tons of bombs apiece in thousand-strong raids. The Battle of Britain had in effect made a Nazi invasion impossible. At the same time, Churchill was gearing up to begin the Battle of Germany, which was waged with growing force over the next four and a half years. It was at this point that he adopted the RAF, got himself made an air commodore, and wore this uniform on public and official occasions more often than any other. Like the siren suit, it was rich in symbolism.

Seventh, though Britain was not in a position to attack Hitler on the Continent, Churchill ensured that powerful blows were struck against his ally Mussolini. The moment it became clear that an invasion of Britain was unlikely (Hitler postponed the invasion indefinitely on September 17, 1940), every available aircraft and tank was sent to the Middle East. Before long, the results came flowing in. Italy's ramshackle empire in East Africa was overrun, and Italian troops surrendered in entire units, often without firing a shot. The British position in Iraq was secured against an Arab uprising, and from that point there was no serious threat to Britain's oil supplies in the Persian Gulf, whereas Hitler was soon driven to manufacturing an inferior form of gasoline known as *ersatz,* one of many German words eagerly adopted by the British (*blitz* was another) as a subtle sign that they were capable of swallowing the enemy: Churchill encouraged the trend—*kaput* became a favorite term of his, and *kamerad,* the German cry of surrender. Britain had already seized France's principal warships or put them out of action. Now the two French protectorates in the Middle East, Syria and the Lebanon, which had opted for Vichy, were occupied. This impressed Turkey, which began to lean toward Britain, a process reinforced by Churchill, who sent Eden (now foreign secretary) out to the area for a visit. "What shall I tell Turkey?" he asked. Churchill replied: "Warn her Christmas is coming."

Eighth, Wavell was encouraged to "go for Musso," as Churchill put it, and eventually did. In January 1941 the Italian Libyan force collapsed and countless prisoners were taken, though Wavell did not pursue the fleeing Italians and take the capital Tripoli, being slow and cautious, characteristics Churchill did not like and which eventually led to his replacement. More to his taste was Admiral Cunningham, who had, he said, "the Nelson Touch." In November 1940 Cunningham's seaplanes sank a third of the Italian fleet in harbor at Taranto, and in March 1941 he won the largest fleet action in European waters at the battle of Cape Matapan. Churchill's reaction was characteristic: "How lucky we are the Italians came in!" These victories made welcome headlines at home and were reinforced by the fact that ships that had taken tanks to Cairo were filled going home by over one hundred thousand Italian prisoners of war. They were promptly put to work on farms where they showed themselves industrious and grateful that they were still alive. They proved mighty popular as visible symbols that Britain would win battles as well as suffer defeats. "Friendly Wops," as Churchill put it, "are good for morale." He began to think of the Mediterranean coast as "the soft underbelly of Europe" and planned to attack it as the easiest way to the Nazi vitals.

Ninth, Churchill was always on the lookout for allies, large or small. That was why when Mussolini, desperate for a victory, invaded Greece in October 1940 and was soundly thrashed, calling desperately to Hitler for help, Churchill was in favor of sending troops to Greece, which he did in March 1941. The majority opinion was against him, the Germans invaded in April, and in due course both Greece and Crete were lost. In the long run, however, Churchill was proved right. By this time, thanks to possession of the Nazi encryption machine Enigma and the British decoding center at Bletchley, he was getting regular intercepts of top-level Nazi messages. This was the most closely guarded secret of the war, and it says a lot for the precautions Churchill personally took, and his own discretion, that the Nazis never suspected their codes were broken and continued to use them to the end. The excerpts persuaded Churchill that Hitler intended to invade Russia in May. By coming to the aid of Italy in Greece, Hitler was forced to postpone the invasion till the second half of June 1941, which in practice made it impossible for him to take Moscow and Leningrad before the winter set in. So the attack on Russia, instead of being a blitzkrieg, became a hard slog. Moreover, his attack on Crete with his prize paratrooper forces proved so costly that he banned their use in the Russian campaign, a serious handicap as it turned out. Primed by the intercepts, Churchill warned Stalin that he was about to be invaded. Stalin took no notice,

suspecting a "capitalist trick" to drag him into the war. When it occurred, Churchill was delighted, and at once reversed his quarter
century of hostility to the Soviet Union. "And why not, after all," he
joked. "If Hitler invaded Hell, at least I would ensure that in the
House of Commons I made a favourable reference to the Devil." So
Russia was warmly welcomed by Churchill as "our new and great
ally." When Hitler failed to demolish the Red Army, as most experts
expected, Churchill's opinion rose. On October 29 he made a rous-
ing speech to the boys of his old school, Harrow:

> Do not let us speak of darker days. Let us rather speak of
> sterner days. These are not dark days: these are great days—
> the greatest days our country has ever lived. And we must all
> thank God that we have been allowed, each of us according
> to our stations, to play a part in making these days memora-
> ble in the history of our race.

A month later Japan attacked Britain and America. Hitler then
made his biggest mistake: quite needlessly he declared war on the
United States. Churchill had been strikingly successful in getting
Roosevelt to send war supplies in growing quantities and on "lend-
lease," for Britain's dollar resources were now exhausted. In a
broadcast to America, on February 9, 1941, he had said, "Give us
the tools, and we will finish the job." But he knew this was over-
optimistic: Britain alone was not capable of crushing Germany.
Now the odds had been changed completely. As he put it, "An eventual Allied victory is odds-on." However, he clinched matters by
persuading Roosevelt and his advisers that priority should be given

to defeating Germany first. This was perhaps the most important act of persuasion in Churchill's entire career, and it proved to be absolutely correct.

Indeed, and this is the tenth point, Churchill had an uncanny gift for getting priorities right. For a statesman in time of war it is the finest possible virtue. "Jock" Colville, his personal secretary, said, "Churchill's greatest intellectual gift was for picking on essentials and concentrating on them." But these essentials were always directed toward the destruction of the enemy. General "Pug" Ismay, his closest military adviser, noted, "He is not a gambler but never shrinks from taking a calculated risk if the situation so demands. His whole heart and soul are in the battle, and he is an apostle of the offensive." He made it clear in his memos that no commander would ever be penalized for an excess of zeal toward the enemy. This was a huge comfort and safeguard for aggressive generals and encouraged the spirit of adventure.

These ten points are essential to answering the question: did Churchill save Britain? The answer must be yes. No one else could have done it. This was what was felt at the time by the great majority of the British people, and it has been since confirmed by the facts and documents at our disposal. By the end of 1940 Britain was secure. By the end of 1941 she was clearly on the winning side. Churchill had done it by his personal leadership, courage, resolution, ingenuity, and grasp, and by his huge and infectious confidence. But it must not be thought that he was just a kind of implacable machine making war. He never lost his humanity. His jokes continued and were repeated in ever-widening circles like stones dropped in a pool, until they became the common currency of wartime Britain. People learned to imitate his speech mannerisms. He was referred to on the bus as "Winnie." Brendan Bracken described how, driving round Hyde Park Corner with Churchill, they came across a man fighting with his wife. The man recognized Churchill, stopped, and took off his hat: "It's the Guv'nor—are you well, sir?"

Churchill also punctuated his grim, endless pursuit of the war by curious acts of kindness. On the evening of May 10, 1940, having just taken office, and while forming his cabinet, he found time to offer asylum to the elderly kaiser, once a friend and now in danger of being made Hitler's propaganda puppet. He was always and thoughtfully generous to former political opponents. By the time of the Battle of Britain, Chamberlain (whom he had insisted on keeping in the government and treating with respect) was ill with terminal cancer. On the day of one of the biggest RAF victories, Churchill telephoned the stricken man to tell him of the number of Nazi aircraft shot down. There is also a record of his taking old Baldwin to lunch and cheering him up. When Beaverbrook, as minister of aircraft production, commandeered everyone's iron gates to be melted down, he specially confirmed that Baldwin's gates at Bewdley, his country house, were not to be spared. Churchill found time to cancel the order. He hardly ever cherished a grudge or a grievance or nursed enmity in his heart. He remembered to thank people for their help, too. Before America entered the war, Churchill made a thrilling broadcast on April 27, 1941, which I remember vividly, saying how important American help was, and that it was being provided "in increasing measure." He ended by quoting Arthur Clough's lines:

For while the tired waves, vainly breaking,
Seem here no painful inch to gain,
Far back through creeks and inlets making
Comes, silent, flooding in, the main.

And not by eastern windows only,
When daylight comes, comes in the light,
In front the sun climbs slow, how slowly,
But westward, look, the land is bright!

This quote had a tremendous impact on the listeners. Before dinner, he telephoned Violet Bonham Carter (née Asquith), who had read him the poem thirty-five years before. He asked, "Did you hear my broadcast?" "Of course I did, Winston. Everyone listens when you speak." He reminded her of her reading him the lines so many years before: "And now I have read them to the nation. Thank you!"

By the end of 1941 Churchill was confident that the war would be won. But there were heavy blows to bear. In some ways the first half of 1942 was the worst period of the war for him, for any disasters due to mistakes could no longer be blamed on anyone else. He blamed himself bitterly for underestimating the power and malevolence of Japan, for allowing two capital ships, *Prince of Wales* and *Repulse,* to be sent to sea without air cover, both being sunk with almost all hands, and for the fall of Singapore. There were disastrous reverses in North Africa, where Field Marshal Erwin Rommel and his Afrika Korps proved, for their numbers, the most successful German army of the entire war. Worst of all there were heavy sinkings of Allied supply ships in the North Atlantic, for which Churchill could not provide the explanation. The truth, we now know, was that Enigma intercepts had been providing information about the positions of U-boats, making them easier to sink, but early in 1942 a change in Nazi coding made this intelligence unavailable for several months, until the Bletchley code breakers caught up.

The concentration of bad news in 1942 led to the most serious challenge Churchill faced in the entire war. Though often criticized by individual MPs, including one heavyweight, Aneurin Bevan—"a squalid nuisance," as Churchill described him—he always won the rare debates by enormous majorities or without a vote. However, early in July, the news that Rommel was only ninety miles from Cairo led to a vote of censure proposed by Sir John Wardlaw-Milne, who was described by Harold Nicolson as "an imposing man with a calm manner which gives an impression of solidity." Hitting hard at Churchill personally, Milne demanded the prime minister be stripped of his position as minister of defense and that it be handed over to "a dominating figure to run the war," and "a generalissimo to command all the armed forces." Who was this to be? Milne announced: "the Duke of Gloucester." This man was the booby younger brother of the king, notorious for his large body and tiny brain. The House shrieked and bellowed with laughter. Churchill was saved—it was the best stroke of pure luck he enjoyed in the war, and remained a delightful national joke for months.

Shortly after the tide turned again. Churchill got himself a winning general in Africa in the shape of Bernard Montgomery, who (like Nelson) also possessed a gift for turning himself into a national hero. He beat Rommel at the decisive battle of El Alamein in November 1942, and this prepared the way for Allied landings in North Africa, which ultimately brought the surrender of three hundred thousand Germans and Italians in Tunisia—the biggest "bag" of the war. Soon thereafter the Russians won the battle of Stalingrad, with the surrender of Hitler's entire Sixth Army. The decoded intercepts were renewed, with a consequent sinking of U-boats, freeing the way for enormous numbers of American supplies and troops to reach Britain, preparing for a landing on the Continent.

By the end of 1942 Churchill, who had been thinking about postwar geopolitics ever since the Battle of Britain had been won, was actively working to create a world capable of containing the power of the Soviet Union. He did this, to the best of his ability, through the summit system, a form of negotiation he loved—the top men face-to-face, surrounded by their staff and experts (he often traveled with eighty people). In 1943 Captain Pim, who ran his map room, calculated that Churchill had already traveled 110,000 miles since the beginning of the war and had spent thirty-three days at sea and fourteen days and three hours in the air, often exposed to real danger. He had to work his aging body hard. He hated having injections, though he joked about them, telling one nurse, "You can use my fingers or the lobe of my ear, and of course I have an almost infinite expanse of arse." His health was on the whole remarkably good, considering his workload, but he suffered from three strokes or heart attacks, bouts of pneumonia, and other ailments. His doctor, Moran, was (after his patient's death) criticized by the Churchill family and other doctors for writing a book, *Winston Churchill: The Struggle for Survival*, describing in detail the threats to his life arising from health problems. But historians think he was quite right to do so: it is a vital part of the story. Moran did a first-class job in keeping Churchill alive, helped by the prime minister's fundamentally strong constitution, amazing powers of recuperation, and will to live. Churchill was indispensable, and those around him did not dare to think of who could take over if he died. The assumption was Eden—an appalling prospect to those familiar with his over-anxiety bordering on hysteria.

Churchill's great strength was his power of relaxation. Sometimes he painted, discovering in the process of one summit Morocco, and above all Marrakech, where the superb Mamounia Hotel was much to his taste. He loved having his womenfolk with him— Clemmie and his daughters, Diana, Sarah, and Mary. Sarah had made an unfortunate marriage to a stand-up comic, Vic Oliver, whom Churchill detested, even after he faded from the scene during the war. At a conference in Cairo, Churchill was recounting his worries to the resident minister of the Mediterranean, Harold Macmillan, who told him, "You are lucky. Things are going well, really. Look at Musso." The Italian dictator was nearing the end of his power. Everything was going wrong. His foreign minister, Count Ciano, who had married Musso's daughter, had been accused of treason and shot. Churchill reflected on Mussolini's plight and then said, "Well, at least he had the pleasure of murdering his son-in-law."

One aspect of his life Churchill had to neglect during the war was Chartwell. The Nazis knew all about it, and its system of three lakes made it an easy target to identify, night or day. So he was able to visit it only twelve times during the six years of the war, a painful loss. Of course he had Chequers, the beautiful house given to the nation for the relaxation of the prime minister in Lloyd George's day. Churchill used it especially for top-level military conferences and receiving American envoys like Harry Hopkins and W. Averell Harriman. He had there an excellent cook and a fine cellar and installed a cinema in the Elizabethan gallery. He liked action movies, such as *Stagecoach* and *Destry Rides Again,* also a favorite of Lord Beaverbrook, who saw it scores of times. One prize movie Churchill hated was *Citizen Kane.* He walked out halfway through in disgust. He also improved the art collection, adding a mouse to a painting of a lion then believed to be by Rubens: "A lion without a mouse? I'll change that. Pray, bring me my paints." Talk at Chequers went on late into the night. Jock Colville said, "No one comes to Chequers to make up for lost sleep." But Chequers, too, was regarded as vulnerable to Nazi raiders on nights with a full moon. So he got hold of Ronald Tree, a Tory MP who owned Ditchley, a spacious and beautiful golden stone house in Oxfordshire. Could he and his staff use it on the dangerous weekends? Tree, half American (his money came from the Marshall Field's department store fortune), with his wife from Virginia, was glad to help. The Churchill circus settled there for a total of fifteen weekends up to March 1942, when the danger from raiders ended. The food was even better than at Chequers, though Churchill once remarked of a sweet course, pushing the plate away, "This pudding has no theme." It was there also that he objected to a secretary's saddling him with the typescript of a dictated memo which included a sentence ending with a preposition. It was a grammatical solecism he hated, and he barked, "Up with this I will not put." He slept in bedroom number one, which has a magnificent four-poster. The house is now a conference center, and I have slept in this bed myself, in Churchillian comfort.

In the second half of the war, confident in its outcome, Churchill was chiefly preoccupied with keeping as close as possible to the United States while steering it in the direction he wanted to go. He was conscious of the huge superiority of American power but hoped by his ingenuity, powers of argument, and skillful use of his prestige—as when he addressed both houses of Congress—to "punch above my weight," a phrase he coined. He gloried in the "special relationship," telling the Commons:

> The British Empire and the United States have to be somewhat mixed up together in some of their affairs for mutual and general advantage. For my own part, looking to the future, I do not view the process with any misgivings. I could not stop it if I wished. No one can stop it. Like the Mississippi, it keeps rolling along. Let it roll. Let it roll on full flood, inexorable, irresistible, to broader lands and better days.

In his dealings with Roosevelt, Churchill had two difficulties. FDR was an anti-imperialist, opposed strongly to Churchill's evident wish to keep colonies ("I have not become the King's First Minister in order to preside over the liquidation of the British Empire," he said in November 1942). He often suspected Churchill of being guided by imperialist motives when all he wanted was to win the war. But generally, if FDR was oversuspicious of Churchill, he was undersuspicious of Stalin. He had no direct experience of Bolshevism, as Churchill had, and did not hate Communism with every fiber of his being, as Churchill did. In meetings with Stalin, especially at Yalta in January 1945, he blocked Churchill's attempts to coordinate Anglo-U.S. policy in advance: he did not wish, said Averell Harriman, to "feed Soviet suspicions that the British and Americans could be operating in concert." Churchill sadly accepted this. As the Red Army began to push the Nazis back in Eastern Europe, he noted:

> It is beyond the power of this country to prevent all sorts of things crashing at the present time. The responsibility lies with the United States and my desire is to give them all the support in my power. If they do not feel able to do anything, then we must let matters take their course.

There were, however, many points on which Britain, under Churchill's leadership, was in a position to influence and even determine events. Where did he succeed, and where did he fail? When was he right and when wrong? He got the Americans to agree to a joint landing in Africa (Operation Torch), which succeeded and led to the surrender of all Axis forces there, as already noted. This was Churchill's doing and led him in turn to the successful invasions of Sicily and Italy, and the Italian decision to make peace and join the Allies. Compare this, though, with Churchill's decision to "roll up Italy," as he put it. He put his old Harrovian friend Field Marshal Alexander, the general he liked most, in charge. But Italy was defended inch by inch by the Germans under Field Marshal Kesselring, the ablest Nazi general of all, and it proved a long and costly campaign. Probably the resources could have been better used elsewhere. Then there was the massive bomber assault of Germany. This was very much Churchill's campaign, and speaking as one who lived through the war in England, I can testify that it was the most popular of all Churchill's initiations. It was one reason his popularity remained high even when things were going badly wrong in other parts of the war, for virtually every day BBC radio was able to announce heavy raids on Germany the previous night. The British public rejoiced at these raids, the heavier the better. Churchill never repudiated the bombing campaign, even after the war, whilst it was heavily criticized on both strategic and humanitarian grounds. But he did not dwell on it either, or stress his personal responsibility for initiating and continuing it. The head of Bomber Command, Air Marshal "Bomber" Harris, was made the hero (or villain) of the assault.

In fact, on February 14, 1942, Harris was directed by the war cabinet that his primary object was the destruction of the morale of German civilians. Churchill wrote this order. The first big raid in accordance with it was on Lübeck on March 28, 1942, the city "burning like kindling," according to the official report. The first thousand-bomber British raid followed on May 30. Churchill was enthusiastic, for at this date the news was bad and bombing was all he had to show. Altogether, bombing used up 7 percent of Britain's total manpower and maybe as much as a quarter of the country's total war production. It killed six hundred thousand German civilians and reduced but could not prevent the expansion of German war production into the second half of 1944. By the end of 1944 bombing was effectively putting the German war economy out of action, but at that point Nazi survival was being decided on the ground anyway. The nearest Harris and Churchill (helped by U.S. air power) came to a strategic victory was on Hamburg, by far the best-protected German city, from July 24 to August 3, 1943. They used the "window" foil device, which confused German radar. On the night of July 27–28, the RAF created temperatures of 800 to 1,000 degrees centigrade over the city, producing colossal firestorm winds. Transport systems of all kinds were destroyed, as were 214,350 homes out of 414,500, and 4,301 out of 9,592 factories. Eight square miles of the city were burned out entirely, and in one night alone up to 37.65 percent of the total population then living in the city were killed. Albert Speer, the war production minister, told Hitler that if another six cities were similarly attacked he could not keep production going. But Britain did not have the resources to repeat raids on this scale in quick succession. The losses in bombers and aircrews were heavy because of Hitler's concentration of fighter squadrons and air defenses to defend his cities. On the other hand, without the British bombing these assets would otherwise have gone to the eastern front. As a result the Germans lost the air war there: by mid-1943, their air superiority had disappeared, and this was a key factor in their losing the ground war, too. These facts tend to be forgotten by those who assert that it was Russia which really defeated Nazi Germany. Without Churchill's bombing campaign, the eastern front would have become a stalemate.

In attacking Germany, Churchill was never held back by humanitarian motives. The destruction of Dresden on the night of February 13–14, 1945, when between 25,000 and 40,000 men, women, and children were killed, was authorized by him personally. The origin of this atrocity was the desire of Churchill and Roosevelt at Yalta in January to prove to Stalin that they were doing their best to help the Russian effort on the eastern front. The Russians had particularly asked for Dresden, a communications center, to be wiped out. When Harris queried the order, it was confirmed direct from Yalta by Churchill and Air Chief Marshal Portal. Would Churchill have used the atomic bomb against Germany, had it been available in time? Undoubtedly. The British nuclear weapons project had begun seriously in March 1940, before he took over supreme command. But he accelerated it in June, when the Military Application of Uranium Detonation Committee (or Maud, as it was called, whimsically, after a Kentish governess) was joined by the French team, which brought with them the world's entire stock of heavy water, 185 kilograms in twenty-six canisters. In the autumn of 1940 Churchill sent a team to Washington headed by Sir Henry Tizard and Sir John Cockcroft, Britain's two leading military scientists, taking with them all Britain's nuclear secrets in a celebrated "black box." At that time Britain was ahead of any other nation in the quest for a nuclear bomb, and moving faster. Churchill was asked to authorize production plans for a separation plant by December 1940. In July 1941 he got the Maud Report, "Use of Uranium for a Bomb," which told him the weapon could be ready by 1943. When America joined the war, Churchill decided that the risk of Nazi raids against a British A-plant was such that it was safer, with the scientific work now complete, for the industrial and engineering work to be done in America. In fact it proved much more difficult, lengthy, and costly than Maud had anticipated. So the first A-bombs were essentially American. If an all-British bomb had been made in time, Churchill would have commanded its use against Germany.

Perhaps his greatest contribution to the successful outcome of the war, at this stage, was his insistence on the right timing for Operation Overlord, the Allied invasion of northwest Europe. This was necessary for the defeat of Germany, and Churchill made sure it worked and was achieved with minimum loss of life for so immense and hazardous an operation. He argued that an opposed air-sea landing against formidable defenses manned by large, prepared German forces was perhaps the most difficult military undertaking of all. With the costly failure of Gallipoli always in his mind, he insisted that D-day should not take place until overwhelming strength was established and there was a near certitude of success. The Russians had asked for the second front to be opened in 1942. The Americans were willing to risk it in 1943. The "dress rehearsal" at Dieppe in 1942, where Allied losses were unexpectedly high, had shown what hazards lay ahead. Churchill's conditions could not be met until the early summer of 1944. Even so, Overlord might have failed or proved extremely costly had not a highly successful deception plan persuading the Germans that the Normandy landings were a feint and that the real invasion was planned for the Pas de Calais area—another idea of Churchill's—prevented a massive German counterattack in the early stages. Thanks to Churchill, and his memories of the Dardanelles, Overlord was a dramatic success. He wished to be present on the first day to enjoy his triumph. It was the last major occasion on which his desire to participate in military action manifested itself. All those concerned in the operation were horrified. Indeed, the desire was foolish in the extreme, a grotesque exhibition of the childish side of his nature. But he persisted, despite unanimous opposition from the service chiefs, the cabinet, his own staff, and the White House. In the end it was only the opposition of King George VI, who said that if his prime minister risked his life he must do so himself, which scotched the plan.

The delay occasioned by Churchill's ensuring the invasion succeeded necessarily meant the Western forces were behind the Russians in pushing into the heart of the Nazi empire. This had grave political consequences. Churchill sought to mitigate them by demanding a full-speed drive to Berlin by the Anglo-American forces. This was supported by Montgomery, the army group commander, who was sure it was possible and would end the war in autumn 1944, with the West in Berlin first. But Eisenhower, the supreme commander, thought it was risky and insisted on a "broad front" advance, which meant that the war continued into the spring of 1945, and that the Russians got to Berlin first—and Prague, Budapest, Vienna, too. In his last weeks of life, FDR, despite Churchill's pleas, did nothing to encourage Eisenhower to press on rapidly. Montgomery wrote sadly: "The Americans could not understand that it was of little avail to win the war strategically if we lost it politically." That was exactly Churchill's view.

But if he was unable to stop Stalin from turning much of Eastern Europe and the Balkans into Soviet satellites, he did snatch one brand from the burning—Greece. He used British troops, against much well-meaning advice, to intervene decisively in the civil war raging there between Communist guerrillas and forces loyal to the Crown. The politics were complex and made it difficult to decide whom to back among the contending loyalist leaders. Eventually Churchill decided in favor of the republican, anti-Communist general Nikolaos Plastiras. He joked, "The evidence shows we must back Plaster-arse. Let us hope his feet are not of clay." "Tommy" Lascelles, King George VI's secretary, remarked, "I would rather have said that than written Gray's *Elegy*."

Churchill also saved Persia by negotiating a highly satisfactory deal with the Russians, which enabled the British eventually to reduce their influence to a minimum. He kept a tight grip on the Persian Gulf and its oil fields. Of course, by saving Greece, he also enabled Turkey to stay beyond the reach of the triumphant Soviet forces. What is more, by picking a first-class general and backing him with adequate forces, Churchill also made a major contribution to victory in the Far East. Field Marshal William Slim was, next to Montgomery, the ablest of the British generals produced by the war. His Fourteenth Army was often called "the Forgotten Army," in contrast to Montgomery's famous Eighth Army. But it was not forgotten by Churchill. With his encouragement and support it conducted a hard and skillful campaign in Burma, ending in complete victory, which did a great deal to restore British prestige so cruelly damaged by the Singapore disaster. Indeed within four years Britain was able to get back Singapore, Malaya, and Hong Kong. Of course the restoration of Britain's power in the Middle East, South Asia, and the Far East could not be permanent. But for most of a generation, and in some cases longer, Britain was able to enjoy the economic advantages brought by her investments in Gulf oil, Malay rubber and tin, and the mercantile wealth of Hong Kong. For this, Churchill's energy, foresight, and ability to seize on the essentials deserve much of the credit.

As the war drew to a close in the early months of 1945, Churchill visibly held back his efforts. His aggressiveness declined. He enjoyed his brief and successful intervention in Greece. But destruction now sickened him. He sent a memo to Harris to slacken off the attack on German cities as opposed to strategic targets; "otherwise," as he put it, "what will lie between the white snows of Russia and white cliffs of Dover?" Much of his imaginative energy was spent in trying to get the sick Roosevelt to do the sensible thing. "No lover," he said, "ever studied every whim of his mistress as I did those of President Roosevelt." The death of FDR, however painful to Churchill, came as a relief, especially as Harry S. Truman, brisk, decisive, much better informed on strategy, proved infinitely easier to deal with. When Churchill was tired, he talked, often off the point. He refused to read his papers. Colville noted on April 26: "The PM's box is in a ghastly state. He does little work and talks far too long, as he did . . . before his Greek adventures refreshed him." The businesslike and monosyllabic Clement Attlee, his deputy premier, sent him a sharp memo of complaint. Churchill is credited with many jokes about the Labour Party leader. "Yes, he is a modest man. But then he has so much to be modest about." "An empty taxi drew up outside the House of Commons, and Mr. Attlee got out." Sometimes they were mean and savage: "Attler, Hitlee." One of Attlee's staff used to whistle, a habit Churchill could not bear. His antipathy to whistling is curiously apt, for Hitler was an expert and enthusiastic whistler: he could do the entire score of *The Merry Widow,* his favorite operetta. It seems expert whistling by music lovers was a feature of pre-1914 Vienna: Gustav Mahler and Ludwig Wittgenstein were whistler maestros.

Tired as he was, Churchill treated the surrender of Germany with suitable rhetoric and champagne popping. He drank a bottle of his prize 1928 vintage Pol Roger. He was relieved by Hitler's suicide. He had not relished the prospective task of hanging him. As Beaverbrook said, "He is never vindictive." His saying had always been—it is one of his best obiter dicta—"In war, resolution. In defeat, defiance. In victory, magnanimity. In peace, goodwill." Magnanimity came naturally to this generous, jovial old man (he was seventy at the end of the war). Lord Longford, the British minister for postwar Germany, showed notable compassion for the German people. Churchill came up to him at a Buckingham Palace garden party and said, slowly, "I am glad that there is one mind suffering for the miseries of the Germans."

Churchill wanted to carry on the coalition until Japan surrendered. But the Labour Party refused. So he formed a Tory government, had Parliament (which was now ten years old) dissolved, and reluctantly began an election campaign. He hit hard, or rather fairly hard, for him. The prevailing wisdom was that he hit too hard, and that his anti-Labour speeches, inspired, it was said, by Lord Beaverbrook, did the Tory cause terrible harm. Nothing could be further from the truth. No one took much notice of opinion polls in those days. In fact Gallup had been predicting a Labour victory for some time by the huge margin of 10 percent: a landslide. Churchill had a good case. After all, if his advice had been taken in the 1930s, the war might have been avoided altogether. By contrast, Labour had opposed rearming Britain right up to the declaration of war. Attlee himself had told the Commons on December 21, 1933, "We are unalterably opposed to anything in the nature of rearmament." Churchill was right to remind voters of these things. There was nothing personal in his criticism. Before the Labour ministers left his government, he gave a party for them and offered a toast. With tears running down his cheeks, he said, "The light of history will shine on all your helmets." The evidence shows that Churchill's speeches reduced the Labour lead to 8.5 percent by polling day. There was a delay between polling and the announcement of the results to allow the voters of the overseas forces to be counted. Few, it is thought, voted against Churchill. The vote was against the Tory Party, or rather against the upper classes, the officer class who spoke in clipped accents, wore cavalry breeches, and drank port after dinner. The result was due to be announced on July 26. The night before, Churchill recorded, he was awoken by a presentiment of disaster: "a sharp stab of almost physical pain." The next day came the news: Labour had won nearly 400 seats, the Conservatives were reduced to 210 seats, and Churchill was out. As he put it:

> On the night of 10 May 1940, at the outset of the mighty Battle of Britain, I acquired the chief power in the State, which henceforth I wielded in ever-growing measure for five years and three months of world war, at the end of which time, all our enemies having surrendered unconditionally or being about to do so, I was immediately dismissed by the British electorate from all further conduct of their affairs.

Mrs. Churchill's comment was: "Perhaps it is a blessing in disguise." To which Churchill replied: "It appears to be very effectively disguised."

Chapter Seven

Glorious Twilight

Clementine Churchill's belief that the 1945 defeat might prove a blessing was abundantly justified, in many different ways. First, it spared her husband the agony of presiding over a dramatic but inevitable contraction of Britain's global power. The country emerged from six years of total war exhausted, impoverished, and emotionally numb. Clement Attlee's Labour government had no inhibitions about giving India its independence. As Churchill had predicted, the vast country split into Hindu and Moslem halves, accompanied by terrible slaughter. But the disintegration he feared did not take place. Indeed, the emergence of India as a great modern economic power, which he believed would take place under British tutelage, eventually began under Indian leadership a generation after his death. An India becoming rich, which Gandhi was sure would destroy her culture and soul, was to Churchill a welcome prospect, a final justification of British rule. So in this respect he was ultimately proved right, and Gandhi wrong. But he was glad he was spared the duty of setting India free. As usual, however, having fought the legislation through all its stages, he accepted the verdict of Parliament. As he said to Nehru, the new Indian prime minister, "It is now your task to lead to prosperity the India I loved and served."

He was also spared the pain of presiding over Israel's birth. A fervent Zionist he remained. Ben-Gurion and Weizmann, the founding fathers, were friends. But he could not bear the savage terrorist campaign waged by Irgun and the Stern Gang and against British troops, which preceded Israel's formation. "I try to put everything concerning Palestine out of my mind," he said sadly.

As he saw it, his main global task during his period of opposition was twofold. First to arouse the world, and especially the United States, to the dangers presented by the power of Stalin's Soviet Union. In America he was universally popular. On March 6, 1946, invited by President Truman, who became a firm friend and a warm admirer, to make a major speech at Westminster College in Fulton, Missouri, his home state, Churchill responded with a call to vigilance in response to the Soviet peril. "An iron curtain has descended across the Continent," he said. Whether he invented the term "iron curtain" is a matter of dispute. He certainly popularized it, as well as "cold war"—"A cold war against Russia has replaced the hot war against Germany," as he put it. But Churchill equally saw his second task was to promote dialogue across the cold war iron curtain. He wanted summits, as always. A favorite saying of his was "Jaw-jaw is better than war-war." He much resented the accusation that he was a man of war, still more a warmonger. In 1941 he allowed himself to be photographed holding a Thompson submachine gun, part of a shipment from America. It was often used against him to illustrate the image of "Gangster Churchill" harped on by Hitler and occasionally by his Labour enemies. But it was a splendid photo, and Churchill loved it. When he made his wartime voyages across the Atlantic by liner, he insisted the lifeboat to which he was assigned be provided with "tommy guns." "I dread capture more than death," he said, "and I will go down fighting."

All the same, he was anxious to lose his reputation for bellicosity. That was why he welcomed the emergence of Ernest Bevin as a tough, resolute, and, if necessary, fierce foreign secretary in 1945, one quite capable of standing up to the Russians and giving them, to use his terminology, "what for." He also applauded Attlee for his firm handling of Soviet forward moves, especially during the Berlin blockade. He disliked belittling remarks about Attlee (except when he made them himself). Once, at Chartwell, Sir John Rodgers referred to Attlee as "silly old Attlee." Churchill exploded:

> Mr Attlee is Prime Minister of England. Mr Attlee was Deputy Prime Minister during the War, and played a great part in winning the War. Mr Attlee is a great patriot. Don't you dare call him "silly old Attlee" at Chartwell or you won't be invited again.

Churchill considered it fortunate that the war in Korea came while Attlee and Labour were still in power. He told a group of Tory MPs early in 1951, "We had no alternative but to fight, but if I had been Prime Minister, they would have called me a warmonger. As it is, I have not been called upon to take so invidious a step as to send our young men to fight on the other side of the globe. The Old Man has been good to me." Sir Reginald Manningham-Buller, MP, was puzzled. "What old man, sir?" Churchill chuckled. "Why, Sir Reginald. Almighty God, the Ruler of the Universe!"

It is likely that the 1945 election result was also a blessing simply in relieving Churchill's workload. If he had carried on as prime minister without a break, he might not have lived long. That was the medical view. As it was, while attending the House of Commons often and making some memorable speeches, he was able to hand over the main business of the Opposition to younger men: Eden, R. A. Butler, Oliver Lyttelton, and Harold Macmillan. He enjoyed many breaks. He took his painting more and more seriously. After his defeat, Field Marshal Alexander placed at his disposal a superb villa his army had commanded overlooking Lake Como, and Churchill set to, to paint the glorious scenery there. The news of his skill as a landscape painter was spreading. The rich began to collect his work. His canvases fetched high prices in the auction rooms. His excellent book *Painting as a Pastime* circulated widely and won the approval of the president of the Royal Academy, Sir Alfred Munnings, who wanted anyone of talent to take up painting and thought Churchill a shining example of how high an amateur could rise with proper encouragement and enthusiasm. He contrived to get Churchill elected an Honorary Member of the Royal Academy Extraordinary. Nothing in Churchill's life gave him greater pleasure. He sent his pictures to the summer exhibition and always, if he could, attended the annual banquet, often speaking there. He and Munnings had a lot in common, especially love of life and color and detestation of "modern art." Munnings related: "Mr. Churchill said to me, 'Alf, if you were walking down Piccadilly, and you saw Picasso walking in front of you, what would you do?' 'Kick his arse, Mr. Churchill.' 'Quite right, Alf.'"

In addition, Churchill took up racing. Clemmie disapproved: "A rich man's sport," she said. "Before he bought the horse (I can't think why) he had hardly been on a racecourse in his life." Actually, the idea came from his son-in-law Christopher Soames, who had married his daughter Mary and who loved racehorses. The old idolization of his father stirred in Churchill's veins: "I can revive my father's racing colours." He did, and set up a small stud near Newchapel Green, convenient for Lingfield races and not far from Chartwell. He acquired (among others) a gray colt called Colonist II, which won thirteen races for him, including some big ones, and proved a popular bet among working-class punters before going out to stud. Churchill was elected to the Jockey Club in 1950 and loved that, too. Moreover, owning racehorses, far from ruining him, actually made him quite a bit of money.

But the chief activity of the postwar Churchill was writing. This is the main reason Clementine was right to say the 1945 defeat was a blessing in disguise. He had always believed—he said so explicitly in May 1938—"Words are the only things that last for ever." Between 1941 and 1945 he had performed great deeds. Now he needed to write the words to ensure that the deeds were correctly described and so made immortal. After the 1945 landslide, he buckled down to the immense and daunting task of writing his war memoirs immediately. The work was pressed forward with all deliberate speed and with all the resources of intellect and energy. Despite its immense length—over 2 million words—the great majority of the book was done by the time he returned to power at the end of 1951. It is a disturbing thought that if he had remained in office it might never have been done at all. If, by carrying on with his overwhelming efforts as premier, especially in the disheartening conditions of the postwar world, he had shortened his life, it would certainly not have been done. The world would have lost a masterpiece, and our view of Churchill might now be distinctly different.

The work was a team effort. Chartwell became a writing factory, with ghostly co-writers, research assistants, historical consultants, and military experts flitting in and out, and with secretaries and typists pounding away by day and taking dictation by night. Churchill called his creative formula "the three Ds—documents, dictation and drafts." The book was a documentary history as well as a personal memoir. He had from an early age always hoarded papers (as did George Washington), and Chartwell had been refashioned by him partly to house this archive efficiently. What he learned from writing *The World Crisis* was the need to make the earliest possible use of official papers, and if possible to get physical possession of them as well as the legal right to use them. From the start in World War II, he applied this lesson assiduously. It is likely that many of his wartime writings—memos, orders, assessments, and strategic directives— were written by him with a view to future use in his memoirs. It was one reason he always gave or confirmed his orders in writing. Before he left Downing Street in summer 1945 he and the then cabinet secretary, Sir Edward Bridges, made what has been called "a remarkable bargain." Churchill asked for no financial, honorific, or other reward for his unique wartime services. What he asked for, and got, was agreement that a vast quantity of the wartime official papers be classified as his personal property. Moreover, he was allowed to remove them to his personal archive at Chartwell. The only qualification was that their publication had to be approved by the government of the day. This bargain meant that Churchill was able to document his account in full from the start. He was right ahead of the field, by miles. There was virtually no competition during the seven years it took him to write and publish the work, especially from the very top. Hitler, Mussolini, and Roosevelt were dead (so were Chamberlain and Baldwin, of course). Stalin wrote no memoirs, thinking—the fool!—that Soviet official history, supervised by him, would do instead. Churchill published well before the various generals, admirals, air marshals, and politicians who had also participated could get their word in. He also benefited from exclusivity. The British documents to which Churchill alone had full access were closed to everyone else except certain authors of official histories on specific and narrow subjects. In 1958 legislation permitted access, subject to the "fifty year rule," which meant any particular document could not be seen by the public for half a century. In 1967 the period was reduced to thirty years, but by then Churchill was dead, having got his word in first.

In effect, the period of revisionism did not start until the decade after Churchill's death. By then many of the verdicts he sought to impose had become deeply embedded in the received version of history, taught in schools and universities, and the heroic epic of Churchill, largely written or inspired by himself, had passed into the public historical memory. Was it truthful? A large proportion of it is documentation, especially the wartime minutes and telegrams. Churchill dictated long passages on key episodes of particular importance to him, which he recalled vividly. There were also extensive drafts, corrected by Churchill, which were written by "the Syndicate," the team of research assistants under the leadership of Bill Deakin, an academic and the only professional historian on the team, Henry Pownall, and Gordon Allen. Experts and participants—service chiefs, industrialists, and scientists—were summoned to help with special passages. All these people served to correct Churchill's memory of events when necessary and to balance his exuberance. But his memory was superlative at this stage of his life and remarkably free from any grudges, let alone malice. The production of the work has been compared to results achieved by a big scientific research group directed by a genius who gets the credit. Asked if Churchill really wrote the book himself, Denis Kelly, office manager of the Syndicate, replied that was like asking a master chef, "Did you cook the whole banquet with your own hands?" A careful study of both the work and the way it was put together may reveal manipulations, omissions, and suppressions (for obvious reasons, little is said of Enigma and successful code breaking such as Ultra). But the impression that emerges is that Churchill was a historian of passion, romantic and often inspired to special insights and near poetry, and a writer of dynamic power and energy, as well as a recording angel of striking ruthlessness. By giving his version of the greatest of all wars, and his own role in it, he knew he was fighting for his ultimate place in history. What was at stake was his status as a hero. So he fought hard and took no prisoners. On the whole he won the war of words, as he had earlier won the war of deeds.

War Memoirs was immensely successful, not least because so much in it was new to the reader, and especially fascinating to those who had lived through the years he described. Indeed it was one of the most popular and highly rewarded books ever published. The original deal of May 1947 covering five volumes brought Churchill $2.23 million, the equivalent of about $50 million today. But he also got huge sums from the *New York Times* and Time Life for serial rights. In 1953 he was awarded the Nobel Prize for Literature, only the second historian to be so honored (the first was Theodor Mommsen, who wrote on ancient Rome). At the time of this prize giving, the *Daily Telegraph* of London, which had serialized the latest volume, stated that volumes one to five had already sold 6 million copies in English and had been serialized in fifty newspapers in forty countries. No book of comparable size—nor many of any size—has so quickly achieved such circulation. The British and American publishers made fortunes from the work, as did Churchill's agent, Emery Reeves. The Churchill family benefited bountifully not only from the work's earnings but also by the bargain over the papers, which were donated to the Chartwell Trust and sold to Lord Camrose of the *Daily Telegraph*. This incorporated a clever legal device to avoid the punitive taxation which would have made the memoirs pointless financially.

Churchill survived the war by twenty years, and spent most of the first decade in active politics. Should he have retired? He thought the people wanted him. They said so, according to the polls. He had always bowed to the popular will when it expressed the national interest. He had said, in 1944, that an electoral defeat might be coming and must be respected: "What is good enough for the people is good enough for me." After resigning the premiership, he moved from Downing Street to Claridge's, until his house was ready, and was observed waiting outside the hotel for his car and singing an old popular song from his youth: "North Pole, South Pole, now I'm up the Pole, since I got the sack, from the Hotel Metropole." At his farewell dinner party at Chequers, where a rehoboam of champagne was drunk, he made some remarks about his future conduct: "I will never give way to self-pity. The new government has a clear mandate which the opposition had no right to attack in principle. The new government will have the most difficult task of any in modern times, and it is the duty of everyone to support them in matters of national interest." Churchill applied these rules to his own conduct as leader of the Opposition. Labour's immense program was vigorously contested, but Churchill never threatened to destroy it if he returned to power. His chief contribution, he felt, was to voice the British view all over the world. So memorable speeches were made before immense audiences. At Zurich, he promoted European unity under Franco-German leadership, a prophetic notion. He stressed the importance of the "spiritual" element in such leadership, an aspect of unity which, alas, has been forgotten. A parliamentarian to the very roots of his political personality, he also stressed the importance of the Strasbourg parliament as opposed to the Brussels bureaucracy. Indeed, on August 11, 1950, he addressed a crowd of over twenty thousand in the open at Place Kléber, Strasbourg. The reception was overwhelming: nothing like it had been seen in the city ever before, or since. But alas here, too, Churchill's wisdom has been ignored and bureaucracy has triumphed in every corner of the European community.

One reason Churchill hung on was that he loved the House of Commons so much. His speeches were still events, eagerly awaited. But there were also unpredictable "outbursts of charm," as the parliamentary diarist "Chips" Channon put it. A sector of far-left Labour MPs disliked him and often subjected him to abuse. Once, when he was leaving the chamber, there were shouts of "Rat!" "Leaving the sinking ship!" "Don't come back!" Churchill paused, turned round, then blew kisses at his assailants. This brought shouts of laughter from all parts of the House. Churchill did not win the 1950 election, but he returned greatly strengthened and full of mischievous glee. When Hugh Gaitskell, then the new chancellor of the exchequer, a "prissy Wykehamist" in Churchill's view, who stood on his dignity a little too often, was making a solemn economic statement, Churchill began to search his pockets for something. First his trousers. Then his jacket. Then his top pocket. Then all his waistcoat pockets. This extensive search gradually attracted the attention of the House. Eventually Gaitskell, aware he had lost his audience, snapped at Churchill in irritation, "Can I help you?" Churchill replied sweetly, "I am only looking for a jujube." Again, there was a roar of laughter from all parties.

At the end of 1951 there was another election, and this time Churchill was returned to office with a majority of seventeen. He quickly formed a government, taking over the defense portfolio himself for a time. Other wartime figures made an appearance: Ismay, Cherwell, the Earl of Woolton, Lord Leathers, Alexander. But increasingly, the main work was done by professional politicians like Eden, Butler, and Macmillan. Churchill was keen to introduce new young talent, employing the graceful manner he brought to even the routine jobs of the prime minister, such as the filling of junior offices. Lord Carrington, a young peer with a good war record in the Guards, was out shooting on his Buckinghamshire estate when a message came to phone Number Ten. On his return he found Churchill on the line. "Been out shooting I hear. Game good?" "Excellent." "I am glad to hear it. Now I want to ask you: would you care to join my shoot?" That was how Carrington became undersecretary for agriculture, the first step in a career which ended as a distinguished foreign secretary. Churchill felt he had no mandate to reverse Labour's nationalization measures, nor to "tame" the unions, nor to abolish the National Health Service, the creation of his old enemy Aneurin Bevan (indeed the two of them were sometimes seen sharing a whiskey and jokes: they were "incapable of resisting each other's charm"). Labour's work was left virtually untouched—Evelyn Waugh complained in his *Diaries,* "The clock has not been put back one single second." There were even complaints that Churchill was slow to end rationing and other wartime egalitarian restrictions which Labour had prolonged. The country had to wait till Margaret Thatcher in the 1980s for the deadly burden of Attlee's "Socialism and Water" to be drained away and replaced by privatization and the profit motive.

Churchill reserved his energy for foreign affairs. While unable to bring about a summit with Russia, he kept the "special relationship" with America in constant repair. He met President Eisenhower in Bermuda and paid an official visit to Washington in June 1954. The young vice president, Richard Nixon, left a vivid verbatim account of his conversation on that occasion covering the French predicament in Vietnam, the war against Communist guerrillas in Malaya, colonialism, imperialism, nuclear weapons, who was running Russia, and many other matters. "He enjoyed himself thoroughly," Nixon wrote, "and was one of those rare great leaders who relished small talk as much as world-shaking issues." Assigned the prestigious Lincoln Bedroom in the White House, where the bed was hard, he crept out in the middle of the night to the so-called Queen's Bedroom, which was empty and where he knew from experience that the bed was luxurious. He told Mrs. Nixon that he had his first whiskey of the day at 8:30 in the morning, but deplored the habit of John Foster Dulles of drinking highballs during dinner: "For the evening is Champagne Time." He joked about Dulles: "The only bull I know who carries his china shop around with him." He said, "That man makes a beautiful declension: 'Dull, Duller, Dulles.'"

In 1953, after long resisting, Churchill allowed the queen to make him a Knight of the Garter. This was a sign he was thinking of retiring, for he had always declined honors which involved a change of name: he valued being "Mr. Churchill." There was a stroke later that year. Recovered, he found reasons for hanging on. He thought Eden "not up to" being prime minister physically and emotionally, but he also felt "he deserves his turn. Who knows? All may be well." In fact, Eden's brief turn ended in the fatal invasion of Egypt and the equally disastrous withdrawal. Churchill commented, "I would have been afraid to go in. But being in, I would have been even more afraid to go out."

Churchill, aged seventy-nine, handed over in April 1955. His last speech had been on March 1, a virtuoso effort he prepared carefully and "dictated every word himself." He said:

Which way shall we turn to save our lives and the future of the world? It does not matter so much to old people; they are going to die soon anyway; but I find it poignant to look at youth in all its activity and ardour and, most of all, to watch little children playing their merry games, and wonder what would lie before them if God wearied of mankind.

However, he added, he was not despondent:

The day may dawn when fair play, love for one's fellow men, respect for justice and freedom, will enable tormented generations to march forth serene and triumphant from the hideous epoch in which we have to dwell. Meanwhile, never flinch, never weary, never despair.

The last ten years of Churchill's life were an age of dying embers, with occasional flickers of flame and fiery glows. He finished his *History of the English-Speaking Peoples*. He painted: "I love the bright colours. I feel sorry for the dull browns." He thought the best thing about heaven would be the infinitely brilliant color scheme. But he also saw the afterlife as "some kind of velvety cool blackness." He then paused. "Perhaps I may be reborn as a Chinese coolie. You know, those were the people employed in South Africa whom I referred to in my first ministerial speech in the Commons. I said that to call them slaves would be to be guilty of a terminological inexactitude. Oh, how glorious English words are! However, if I am reborn a coolie, I shall lodge a strong protest at the Bar of Heaven."

Much of his time was spent in the south of France, at the villa of Emery Reeves, whose pretty wife fussed over him enjoyably. There were many other houses open to him there, notably Beaverbrook's

La Capponcina, which was put at his disposal six months of the year. He made the acquaintance of Aristotle Onassis, the Greek shipowner, and went for eight cruises in all on his capacious and luxurious yacht, the *Christina*. Churchill was particularly fond of it because it was a converted destroyer with huge, fast engines. For a time he was still adventurous. There is a vignette of him insisting on descending to a Mediterranean beach by a rocky cliff, and then being unable to climb up it again. He had to be hauled up (all five foot seven of him, and 154 pounds) in a bosun's chair, pulled by a gang of fellow guests which included the ravishing Lady Diana Cooper and the ballet star Margot Fonteyn.

In his eighties Churchill was often forgetful, deaf, and lost in thought. The writer James Cameron, who had dinner *à trois* with Churchill and Beaverbrook at La Capponcina, describes a silent meal. Suddenly Churchill asked, "Ever been to Moscow, Max?"— "Moscow" pronounced to rhyme with "cow." "Yes, Sir Winston— you sent me there, remember?" Churchill went back into silence. At the end of the evening, saying good-bye, Cameron in his nervousness grasped Churchill's hand too roughly. The old man reacted with fury, blue eyes blazing: "Goddamn you!"

Churchill often stayed at the Hôtel de Paris in Monte Carlo, in a penthouse flat prepared for him. But he liked to dine downstairs with Mrs. Reeves, known as "Rhinestone Wendy." Evelyn Waugh, also staying there, wrote to Ian Fleming's wife, Ann:

We sometimes see Sir Winston (at a respectful distance) gorging vast quantities of rich food. His face is elephant grey and quite expressionless. His moll sits by him coaxing him and he sometimes turns a pink little eye towards her without turning his head.

He had a bad fall at the hotel, and that was the beginning of the end. He had been reelected to the Commons in 1959, though he never spoke thereafter, and paid his last visit to the place he loved on July 27, 1964. He celebrated his ninetieth birthday in November and died the following January, the twenty-fourth. His final days were painless and without incident. His last words were: "I am bored with it all." But then he added, looking at the faces around his bedside, "The journey has been enjoyable and well worth making—once!"

Epilogue

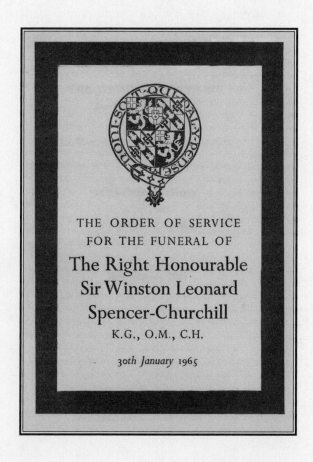

THE ORDER OF SERVICE
FOR THE FUNERAL OF

The Right Honourable
Sir Winston Leonard
Spencer-Churchill

K.G., O.M., C.H.

30th January 1965

On January 27, 1965, Churchill's coffin was taken from his house in Hyde Park Gate to Westminster Hall, where it lay in state. Over three hundred thousand people filed slowly past the catafalque. At 9:45 on January 30 the coffin was taken from Westminster to St. Paul's on a gray gun carriage last used at the funeral of Queen Victoria. The state funeral ordered by Parliament was the first for a politician since Gladstone's. But in its somber magnificence its only precedent was the burial of the Duke of Wellington in 1852. From the funeral, attended by the queen, five other monarchs, and fifteen heads of state, the coffin went across the Thames by boat, then from Waterloo Station by train to Long Hanborough, the nearest station to Bladon, parish church of Blenheim Palace. Churchill was buried in the churchyard next to his father and mother and his brother, Jack, less than a mile from the room in the palace where he was born.

In his ninety years, Churchill had spent fifty-five years as a member of Parliament, thirty-one years as a minister, and nearly nine years as prime minister. He had been present at or fought in fifteen battles, and had been awarded fourteen campaign medals, some with multiple clasps. He had been a prominent figure in the First World War, and a dominant one in the Second. He had published nearly 10 million words, more than most professional writers in their lifetime, and painted over five hundred canvases, more than most professional painters. He had reconstructed a stately home and created a splendid garden with its three lakes, which he had caused to be dug himself. He had built a cottage and a garden wall. He was a fellow of the Royal Society, an Elder Brother of Trinity House, a Lord Warden of the Cinque Ports, a Royal Academician, a university chancellor, a Nobel Prizeman, a Knight of the Garter, a Companion of Honour, and a member of the Order of Merit. Scores of towns made him an honorary citizen, dozens of universities awarded him honorary degrees, and thirteen countries gave him medals. He hunted big game and won a score of races. How many bottles of champagne he consumed is not recorded, but it may be close to twenty thousand. He had a large and much-loved family, and countless friends.

So Winston Churchill led a full life, and few people are ever likely to equal it—its amplitude, variety, and success on so many fronts. But all can learn from it, especially in five ways.

The first lesson is: always aim high. As a child Churchill received no positive encouragement from his father and little from his mother. He was aware of failure at school. But he still aimed high. He conquered his aversion to math, at least enough to pass. He reinforced success in what he could do: write a good English sentence. Conscious of his ignorance, he set himself to master English history and to familiarize himself with great chunks of literature. Once his own master, he played polo to win the top award in the world. He got himself into five wars in quick succession and became both a veteran of military lore and one of the world's most experienced (and highly paid) war correspondents. Then he set his sights on the House of

Commons and stayed there (with one lapse) for over half a century. He sought power and got it in growing amplitude. He never cadged or demeaned himself to get office, but obtained it on his own terms. He sought to be prime minister feeling only he could achieve certain things. In 1940 he aimed not only high but at the highest—to rescue a stricken country in danger of being demoralized, to put it firmly on its feet again, and to carry it to salvation and victory. He did not always meet his elevated targets, but by aiming high he always achieved something worthwhile.

Lesson number two is: there is no substitute for hard work. Churchill obscured this moral by his (for him) efficient habit of spending a working morning in bed, telephoning, dictating, and consulting. He also manifestly enjoyed his leisure activities, for him another form of hard work, to keep himself fit and rested and to enable himself to do his job at the top of his form. The balance he maintained between flat-out work and creative and restorative leisure is worth study by anyone holding a top position. But he never evaded hard work itself: taking important and dangerous decisions, the hardest form of work there is, in the course of a sixteen-hour day. Or working on a speech to bring it as near perfection as possible. No one ever worked harder than Churchill to make himself a master orator. Or forcing himself to travel long distances, often in acute discomfort and danger, to meet the top statesmen face-to-face where his persuasive charm could work best. He worked hard at everything to the best of his ability: Parliament, administration, geopolitics and geostrategy, writing books, painting, creating an idyllic house and garden, seeing things and if possible doing things for himself. Mistakes he made, constantly, but there was never anything shoddy or idle about his work. He put tremendous energy into everything, and was able to do this because (as he told me) he conserved and husbanded his energy, too. There was an extraordinary paradox about his white, apparently flabby body and the amount of muscle power he put into life, always.

Third, and in its way most important, Churchill never allowed mistakes, disaster—personal or national—accidents, illnesses, unpopularity, and criticism to get him down. His powers of recuperation, both in physical illness and in psychological responses to abject failure, were astounding. To be blamed for the dreadful failure and loss of life in the Dardanelles was a terrible burden to carry. Churchill responded by fighting on the western front, in great discomfort and danger, and then by doing a magnificent job at the ministry of munitions. He made a fool of himself over the abdication and was howled down by a united House of Commons in one of the most savage scenes of personal humiliation ever recorded. He scrambled to his feet and worked his way back. He had courage, the most important of all virtues, and its companion, fortitude. These strengths are inborn but they can also be cultivated, and Churchill worked on them all his life. In a sense his whole career was an exercise in how courage can be displayed, reinforced, guarded and doled out carefully, heightened and concentrated, conveyed to others. Those uncertain of their courage can look to Churchill for reassurance and inspiration.

Fourth, Churchill wasted an extraordinarily small amount of his time and emotional energy on the meannesses of life: recrimination, shifting the blame onto others, malice, revenge seeking, dirty tricks, spreading rumors, harboring grudges, waging vendettas. Having fought hard, he washed his hands and went on to the next contest. It is one reason for his success. There is nothing more draining and exhausting than hatred. And malice is bad for the judgment. Churchill loved to forgive and make up. His treatment of Baldwin and Chamberlain after he became prime minister is an object lesson in sublime magnanimity. Nothing gave him more pleasure than to replace enmity with friendship, not least with the Germans.

Finally, the absence of hatred left plenty of room for joy in Churchill's life. His face could light up in the most extraordinarily attractive way as it became suffused with pleasure at an unexpected and welcome event. Witness that delightful moment at Number Ten when Baldwin gave him the exchequer. Joy was a frequent visitor to Churchill's psyche, banishing boredom, despair, discomfort, and pain. He liked to share his joy, and give joy. It must never be forgotten that Churchill was happy with people. He insisted that the gates of Chartwell should always be left open so that the people of Westerham were encouraged to come in and enjoy the garden. He got on well with nearly everyone who served him or worked with him, whatever their degree. Being more than half American, he was never class-conscious. When an old man, his bow to the young queen was a work of art: slow, dignified, humble, and low. But he was bowing to tradition and history more than to rank. He showed the people a love of jokes, and was to them a source of many. No great leader was ever laughed at, or with, more than Churchill. He loved to make jokes and contrived to invent a large number in his long life. He collected and told jokes, too. He liked to sing. Beaverbrook said: "He did not sing in tune but he sang with energy and enthusiasm." He liked to sing "Ta-ra-ra-Boom-de-ay," "Daisy, Daisy," and old

Boer War songs. His favorite was "Take a Pair of Sparkling Eyes" from Gilbert and Sullivan's *The Gondoliers,* which Lady Moran, who had a fine voice, would sing to him. He was emotional, and wept easily. But his tears soon dried, as joy came flooding back. He drew his strength from people, and imparted it to them in full measure. Everyone who values freedom under law, and government by, for, and from the people, can find comfort and reassurance in his life story.

Further Reading

Winston Churchill's life is better documented than any other in the twentieth century. Like Washington, he kept everything from an early age. So did other people. As Kenneth W. Rendell, the greatest living authority on autographs and holographs, says, "Churchill's appeal [to collectors] cannot be overstated." The only comparable figure is Napoleon. There are immense Churchill archives at Chartwell; Churchill College, Cambridge; the British Museum; and other centers. New documents and bits of information are always turning up. Every new book on Churchill tends to be slightly out of date before the author has finished writing it, let alone before it is published. I have written about Churchill myself already, most recently in an essay in *Heroes,* but even my short account contains new items. The eight-volume official biography, the first two volumes by his son, Randolph, the rest by Martin Gilbert, is an exemplary narrative life, which is amplified by a score of supplementary volumes of letters and documents. The whole work is now being reissued, enlarged, corrected, and completed by Hillsdale University Press. Gilbert has also published a number of other valuable books about Churchill. There are many biographies, big and small, and hundreds of books on specialist subjects. The best one-volume biography I have read is by Roy Jenkins. This one-thousand-page volume was written by the late Lord Jenkins when he was eighty, and I salute his

Churchillian energy and endurance. Two other books which I particularly value are Lady Violet Bonham Carter's *Winston Churchill as I Knew Him* and Lord Moran's *Winston Churchill: The Struggle for Survival*. But both contain errors. Indeed, all books about Churchill are fiercely challenged as to facts and judgments in this highly competitive industry. *Churchill by Himself: The Life, Times and Opinions of Winston Churchill in His Own Words,* edited by Richard M. Langworth (London, 2008), corrects many common errors about his jokes and sayings, though I do not agree with it on every point. In addition to Chartwell, Churchill's war rooms in Whitehall are now open to the public. There are many Churchill societies and newsletters, especially in the United States, and regular organized tours to places connected with Churchill. Few people who knew him well are left alive, and those who met him, as I did, are a rapidly dwindling band. But people will be writing about him in a thousand years' time, such is the magic of the man and his doings.

About the Photographs

Frontispiece—1916 portrait of Winston Churchill by the painter William Orpen, widely considered one of the best likenesses ever painted.

(Reproduced with permission of Curtis Brown Ltd, London, on behalf of the Estate of Winston Churchill. Copyright © Winston S. Churchill)

Page 1—Winston Churchill, ca. 1880.

(Reproduced with permission of Curtis Brown Ltd, London, on behalf of the Estate of Winston Churchill)

Page 17—Winston Churchill in 1908, a week before his marriage to Miss Clementine Hozier.

(Library of Congress, New York World-Telegram & Sun Collection)

Page 45—October 1, 1919. Winston Churchill at the Tank Enquiry at Lincoln's Inn.

(Topical Press Agency/Getty Images)

Page 73—Winston Churchill on his way to Buckingham Palace to receive the seals of the office of chancellor of the exchequer from King George V in 1924.

(Library of Congress)

Page 89—Winston Churchill, a keen bricklayer, at work on the wall around his home at Chartwell in Kent, ca. 1930.

(Chris Ware/Keystone/Hulton Archive/Getty Images)

Page 107—June 6, 1941. Winston Churchill watches the arrival of the first B-17 Flying Fortress.
(Library of Congress)

Page 141—December 11, 1955. Sir Winston Churchill flashes his famous V for victory sign on the eve of the general election.
(Bettmann/Corbis)

Page 158—February 1946. Winston Churchill at his easel.
(Bettmann/Corbis)

Page 159—Winston Churchill died on January 24, 1965—seventy years to the day after his father.
(Library of Congress, Earl Warren Papers)

Index

and Clementine, *see* Churchill,
Clementine
and cold war, 144
and Colonial Office, 61, 62
on conservation of energy, 5, 13,
84, 164
dark moods of ("Black Dog"), 7
difficulty of classification, 21–22
election loss (1945) of, 140, 145–46,
147, 151
and empire, 19–20, 130, 137
energy of, 15, 113–14, 127, 163–64
English-language fluency of,
10–11, 24, 75, 129, 162
farewell dinner party for, 151–52
fearlessness of, 35–36, 88
and financial matters, 16, 25, 57,
70, 84–86, 87, 103
as first lord of the Admiralty,
37–43, 48–50, 53, 80, 103–4
funeral service for, 159, 161
and gold standard, 76–77
health concerns of, 4, 65–66,
87–88, 127–28, 146, 155, 158
as home secretary, 31–37
honors and awards to, 151, 155, 162
and horse racing, 146–47, 162
as indispensable, 128
influence of, 131–37
Knight of the Garter, 155, 162
in later years, 156–58
legacy of, 3, 147
legislative accomplishments of,
28–29
lessons learned from, 162–66
life patterns of, 13, 69–70, 83–84
medals awarded to, 13, 14, 16, 21
outspokenness of, 20, 71, 111
painting as pastime for, 55–56, 83,
91, 128, 146, 156
personal traits of, 4–5, 16, 22, 83,
123–24, 137–39, 164–65
political enemies of, 16, 20, 33, 35,
41, 66, 126, 144, 152–53

and political parties, 22–23, 59,
71–72, 139–40
postwar activities of, 151–56
as prime minister, 105–6, 109, 110,
138, 140
as public speaker, 6, 16, 21,
29–30, 66, 71–72, 75, 80, 84, 85,
100–101, 111–12, 114–17, 144, 152,
155–56, 163
radio broadcasts by, 104, 115–16,
122, 124–25
recuperative powers of, 164
reinstatement of, 103–4, 147,
153–55
reputation of, 110, 113, 145
schooling of, 9–11
as secretary of state for war and
air, 117, 164
singing, 165–66
socializing, 37–38
and summit system, 127, 144
and sympathy for the underdog,
20–21, 28
and trade unions, 78–81
travels of, 127, 163
as undersecretary to the colonies,
23–25
uniforms worn by, 113–14, 119
V for victory sign, 117
on war, 21, 47–50, 111–12; *see also*
specific wars and battles
Churchill, Sir Winston Leonard
Spencer, books by:
Aftermath, 67
and documentation, 148–49
*History of the English-Speaking
Peoples,* 156
Ian Hamilton's March, 16
income from, 11, 67, 85, 150–51
*London to Ladysmith via
Pretoria,* 16
Lord Randolph Churchill, 26
My African Journey, 25, 26
Nobel Prize for, 151, 162

About the Author

Paul Johnson is an acclaimed historian whose many bestselling books—including *Napoleon, Modern Times, A History of the American People*, and *A History of Christianity*—have been translated into numerous languages. A frequent contributor to publications such as *The New York Times, The Wall Street Journal*, and *The Spectator*, he lives in London.

DATE		
JAN 1 3 2010		
JAN 1 9 2010		
FEB 0 7 2010		
2-16-2010		
MAY 0 7 2010		
JUN 0 7 2010		
JUN 2 5 2010		